Healthcare Provider's Manual for
Basic Life Support

 American Heart Association

Editors

Ramiro Albarran-Sotelo, MD
Youngstown, Ohio

Loring S. Flint, MD
Chicago, Illinois

Karen J. Kelly, RN, MSEd
Washington, DC

Contributing Editors

James M. Atkins, MD
Dallas, Texas

Leon Chameides, MD
Hartford, Connecticut

C. P. Dail, Jr.
Washington, DC

Judith H. Donegan, MD, PhD
San Francisco, California

Frank X. Doto, MS
Randolph, New Jersey

Thomas J. Herrin, MD
Jackson, Mississippi

William H. Montgomery, MD
Honolulu, Hawaii

Joseph Ornato, MD
Richmond, Virginia

John A. Paraskos, MD
Worcester, Massachusetts

Diane Reid, REMT-P
Dallas, Texas

Prepared under the direction of the
Basic Life Support Working Group, 1984–1987

Chairman
Ramiro Albarran-Sotelo, MD

Members
Loring S. Flint, MD
Thomas J. Herrin, MD
Karen J. Kelly, RN, MSEd

William H. Montgomery, MD
Joseph Ornato, MD
John A. Paraskos, MD

Subcommittee on Emergency Cardiac Care, 1984–1987

Chairwoman
Judith H. Donegan, MD, PhD

Members
Ramiro Albarran-Sotelo, MD
Allan S. Jaffe, MD

Joseph Ornato, MD
John A. Paraskos, MD

© 1988, 1990 American Heart Association

ISBN 0-87493-602-0

Preface

This manual is provided as a reference resource and textbook for the American Heart Association's "Course C: Basic Life Support for Healthcare Providers." Healthcare providers include physicians, nurses, EMTs and allied health personnel. This manual is adapted from the *Instructor's Manual for Basic Life Support*.

Chapters 1 and 2 of the manual are devoted to background — the history and relevance of CPR, the role of the American Heart Association, and other general topics. A detailed presentation of cardiorespiratory anatomy and function is also included, along with a review of the causes of cardiovascular disease and cardiac arrest. Special interest information such as that on epilepsy and stroke is provided but is not a requirement for BLS courses.

Chapters 3–9 provide detailed explanations of the technical aspects of CPR, with separate chapters devoted to each recue situation — adult one-rescuer CPR, foreign body airway obstruction management, pediatric CPR, etc. Chapter 9 deals with special situations, special techniques, and complications in the delivery of CPR.

Chapter 10 is about safety in CPR. It includes information on avoiding cross contamination in manikin practice and rescuer safety in the actual performance of CPR.

Finally, support materials are provided in three appendices, with the course curriculum and the written test and skills performance requirements for course completion outlined in Appendix B.

Table of Contents

History, Concepts, and Systems of Emergency Cardiac Care

One of the most startling ideas of modern medicine is that "sudden death" can be reversed. Perhaps more astonishing is the realization that this miracle of science can be brought about by *any of us, anywhere,* using only our hands, our lungs, and our brains. Cardiopulmonary resuscitation (CPR) that is performed properly and promptly — i.e., before "sudden death" has resulted in final, biological death — can give victims the time to receive treatment by advanced medical techniques.

In 1984 cardiovascular disease accounted for 986,400 deaths, including 540,400 due to heart attacks, most of which were sudden deaths.[1] Communities with large numbers of laypersons trained in basic life support (BLS) and with a rapid response system of well-trained paramedical persons have demonstrated that more than 40% of patients with documented, out-of-hospital ventricular fibrillation (a chaotic, uncoordinated quivering of the heart muscle) can be successfully resuscitated if cardiopulmonary resuscitation (CPR) is provided promptly and followed by advanced cardiac life support.[2] Successful resuscitation in selected subgroups of patients with documented cardiac arrest can be accomplished in 60–80% of cases.[3, 4] In the absence of prompt bystander CPR, though, successful resuscitation of the out-of-hospital cardiac arrest victim may be less than half as likely, despite the availability of a well-trained paramedical team with a rapid response time.[5] Thus, the role of a bystander is indispensable for optimal resuscitative efforts on behalf of the out-of-hospital cardiac arrest victim.[5] Full implementation of community lifesaving systems might save between 100,000 and 200,000 lives each year in the United States.

This chapter presents the historical background for CPR, the philosophy of the current BLS standards, the role of the American Heart Association (AHA) in emergency cardiac care, the structure of AHA training systems in BLS, and the rationale for widespread CPR training. It should provide information for a better understanding of the current AHA position on CPR. The healthcare provider in a BLS course will not be tested on the information in this chapter.

("BLS" and "CPR" are often used interchangeably; however, CPR is a component of emergency cardiac care that may be required in *advanced* cardiac life support as well as in *basic* life support, which are the two levels of emergency cardiac care.)

Historical Perspective

Twenty-five years have passed since the introduction of external chest compressions[6] provided real hope for preventing a substantial number of the nearly 1,000 pre-hospital sudden deaths occurring each day in the United States. In 1966 a National Academy of Sciences–National Research Council (NAS–NRC) conference on CPR recommended that medical and allied health professionals be trained in the external chest compression and exhaled air ventilation (e.g., mouth-to-mouth resuscitation) techniques according to the standards of the AHA.[7, 8] That resulted in widespread acceptance of CPR among healthcare professionals. Nevertheless, training was not prevalent in most parts of the country, and laypersons were usually limited to involvement on a supervised trial basis. During the period 1966–1973, advances toward implementation were made by the AHA through its training materials and programs,[9–15] by the NAS–NRC through its publications,[7, 8, 16–21] by the reports of the Inter-Society Commission for Heart Disease Resources,[22–28] and by the recommendations and evaluations of governmental agencies,[29–34] professional medical societies,[35–39] and private groups.[40-46]

1973 National Conference Recommendations

In 1973 a national conference on standards for CPR and emergency cardiac care (ECC), cosponsored by the AHA and the NAS–NRC, made the following recommendations:

1. Cardiopulmonary resuscitation training programs must be extended to the general public.
2. Training in CPR and ECC must be in accordance with the standards of the AHA, and the AHA should continue to review scientific data and clinical experience and revise and update the standards on those bases.
3. Course completion at various levels of life support must be based on nationally standardized curricula that include written and performance (skills) tests.
4. Delivery of basic and advanced life support by highly trained personnel must be required for all life support units and hospitals on an integrated, stratified, community-wide basis.
5. These goals must be implemented, by legislation and medicolegal action where needed, to ensure the delivery of effective CPR and ECC to the entire population.
6. Recognition of early warning signs of a heart attack and emphasis on prompt access to the emergency medical services (EMS) system should be included in the definition of ECC.

In addition, the national conference defined 1) the role of the American Red Cross (ARC) and other agencies in training the lay public, 2) the role of life support units, or emergency care units, in stratified systems providing ECC, and 3) possible approaches to problems in medicolegal aspects of CPR and ECC.

The recommendations and specific standards for both basic and advanced cardiac life support were published as a supplement to The Journal of the American Medical Association (JAMA)[46] in February 1974. Subsequently, materials for teaching CPR to laypersons and medical professionals, developed primarily by the AHA and the ARC, were widely distributed. As a result, public awareness of CPR was heightened, and interest in CPR training surged. By 1977, 66% of American adults knew of the existence of CPR procedures.[47]

Two national conferences cosponsored by the AHA — Medicolegal Implications of Emergency Medical Care (1975)[48] and Emergency Airway Management (1976)[49] — emphasized CPR training further.

1979 National Conference Recommendations

The charges to the 1979 National Conference to review and revise the 1974 standards for both BLS and advanced cardiac life support (ACLS) involved consideration of 1) then-present recommendations for each level of advanced cardiac life support CPR-ECC (as applied to both children and adults) and the validity of those recommendations based on both clinical experience and scientific data, 2) new scientific data for its potential contribution, 3) areas of promising research in CPR-ECC, and 4) development of state-of-the-art standards and guidelines for the performance of CPR-ECC.

The conference was aware that its first responsibility to the worldwide enthusiasm for and growing success of CPR-ECC was to do no harm. The conference also realized that any substantive change in BLS would require several years to implement. At the same time, the conference recognized its responsibility to recommend new techniques parallel with present BLS teaching if such techniques promised advances in lifesaving potential.

Accordingly, the attitude of the 1979 conference, especially for performance of BLS, was as follows: 1) No changes should be recommended unless unequivocal advantages had been documented. 2) In view of the success of layperson CPR, any new technique offering additional lifesaving potential should be introduced parallel with present recommendations as an alternative technique. 3) If scientific support for any currently recommended procedure is meager, this reality should be cited, recommendations by the conference should be made accordingly, and recommendations for development of a solid data base should be made along with performance recommendations.

As a result of this process, the 1979 conference did not recommend major changes but redefined some terms and expanded certain BLS procedures, particularly for airway management, pediatric resuscitation, and foreign body airway obstruction.[50]

1985 National Conference Recommendations

The objectives of the 1985 National Conference[51, 52] were 1) to review and revise past conference recommendations in light of new scientific and clinical data, 2) to provide prevention recommendations for CPR-ECC programs, 3) to make recommendations regarding education and evaluation needs, including the effectiveness of teaching and the target population for CPR-ECC programs, 4) to provide guidelines for evaluating CPR-ECC outcome, 5) to identify needed CPR-ECC research, and 6) to identify mechanisms by which CPR-ECC can be withheld and/or ACLS withdrawn in appropriate circumstances.

The conference recognized a responsibility to make recommendations based on science and/or clinical data accumulated since 1979. In some subject areas sound data had accumulated, and changes were recommended on that basis. In other areas, while the experimental data were not conclusive, changes were recommended on the basis of clinical evidence or to improve educational efficacy. In still other areas the indications for change were equivocal, and no changes were made. Finally, because of accumulated field and teaching experience, a logical transition was made from some parallel recommendations of 1979 to single therapeutic modalities or treatments in 1985.

The scientist and educator participants of the Conference subjected each proposed change to the above criteria prior to reaching a consensus. Final decisions took into account not only which technique or adjunct or therapy was the most correct but also how the public could best be served, which brought into the decision-making such factors as safety, effectiveness, teachability, and ease of sequencing into related maneuvers. In addition, some recommendations, though remaining basically intact, have since been modified slightly by the peer review process and by integration with other panel recommendations.

Standards and Successful Course Completion in Basic Life Support

Standards and Guidelines

The importance of clarifying what "standards" and "guidelines" are intended to mean was recognized as an important responsibility for the 1979 conference. The term "standards" had been used to apply to the contents of the *JAMA* supplement "Standards for Cardiopulmonary Resuscitation (CPR) and Emergency Cardiac Care (ECC)," published in 1974. The term was employed at that time to introduce the first standardized body of information on the state of the art in BLS and ACLS. Virtually complete acceptance of the recommendations and conceptual material contained within the 1974 standards resulted in the development of teaching materials by different agencies, particularly the ARC and the AHA, which were for the most part consistent, thus minimizing the possibility of public confusion.

As in other fields needing quality control, in BLS training there are "strict constructionists" and "loose constructionists." Strict constructionists require rigid standards for teaching, testing, performance, successful course completion, and renewal, insisting that only in this manner can quality be maintained. Loose constructionists, while realizing the need for uniformity and consistency of content and method in teaching and testing, believe that more flexibility is needed — for two principal reasons: 1) New knowledge and innovation are ongoing, and failure to permit flexibility could result in delay of potentially lifesaving advances. 2) The physician prerogative for discretionary action may be threatened by overly rigid standards, particularly because the term "standards" has important legal as well as medical overtones.

With an eye to maintaining continuity, and because of what is intended and what is not intended by "standards" in BLS and ACLS, the 1980 and 1986 *JAMA* publications were titled "Standards and Guidelines."[50, 51] "Standards" now clearly applies to BLS teaching, especially with regard to laypersons, while "standards" or "guidelines" may be used interchangeably with reference to ACLS, possibly depending on whether one is a strict or loose constructionist.

The 1980 standards and guidelines are intended to

1. Identify the knowledge and performance skills that are commonly necessary for the successful treatment of cardiac arrest victims or the victims of serious or life-threatening cardiac or pulmonary disturbances
2. Indicate that the knowledge and skills recommended or defined do not represent the only medically or legally acceptable approach to a designated problem but an approach that is generally regarded as having the best likelihood of success in view of present knowledge
3. Provide a uniform basis for teaching, testing, and maintaining quality control in BLS and ACLS on the local and national levels
4. Stimulate the widest possible dissemination of not only the knowledge and skills of CPR but also the knowledge of risk reduction and primary prevention, to the largest number of persons possible
5. Provide to the public, to the extent possible, a single approach to the performance of CPR

The standards and guidelines are not intended to imply that 1) justifiable deviations from suggested standards by physicians qualified and experienced in CPR and ECC under appropriate circumstances represent a breach of a medical standard of care, or that 2) new knowledge, new techniques, clinical or research data, clinical experience, or clinical circumstances may not provide sound reasons for alternative approaches to CPR and ECC before the next definition of national standards.

Successful Course Completion

The words "certified" or "certification" are not used to describe completion of the BLS course or the document issued for successful completion of the course. The American Heart Association does not purport to warrant future BLS performance by a Provider or to provide a license of any type for completion of the course.[53]

Because misunderstanding has resulted in some quarters from the use of the term "certified" as it has been applied to BLS, the expression "successfully completed" should be used. It should be understood that the cognitive and performance (skills) testing requirement is the same for each designation.

The Ultimate Coronary Care Unit

Approximately 60% of deaths due to acute myocardial infarction (heart attack) take place outside of the hospital and usually occur within two hours after the onset of symptoms.[54-61] Thus, "sudden death" from coronary heart disease is the most prominent medical emergency today. It is possible that a large number of these deaths can be prevented by prompt, appropriate treatment, which may provide either early entry into the EMS system or cardiopulmonary support using CPR.[4, 62-66]

It has been suggested that the community has the potential for being recognized as the ultimate coronary care unit.[50] With the current interest in CPR, the community may be the ideal mechanism for the control of coronary heart disease (CHD) morbidity and mortality. According to a 1983 Gallup poll, an estimated two thirds of the adult population indicated an interest in being trained in CPR. The proportion of those adults who knew about CPR increased from 66% in 1977 to 87% in 1983, "an extraordinarily high awareness figure."[67] CPR classes should incorporate education in primary prevention (preventing the development of coronary artery disease by, for example, risk factor detection and modification) and secondary prevention (preventing sudden death and myocardial infarction in patients known to have CHD), along with ECC education and training. It is becoming increasingly evident that coronary artery disease (CAD) is born in the community and then nurtured there, beginning with the nutritional patterns of the very young, the pro-smoking messages to teenagers, and the cultural and social pressures that mold unhealthy behaviors. While controversy continues as to the potential impact of risk factor reduction on CHD incidence, there are persuasive data in support of aggressive community action. It is clear, for example, that young and middle-aged men who stop smoking have a major reduction in rates of CHD as compared with those who continue to smoke.[68, 69]

By providing, through education, a mechanism for unprecedented community penetration, CPR may serve as a means of shifting the responsibility for CHD from health-care providers and discrete centers to the community, where CHD is nurtured and where myocardial infarction and sudden death occur with the greatest frequency.

Since one aspect of the ultimate coronary care unit, i.e., layperson CPR, has grown with increasing success, aspects that optimize *preventive* efforts may profitably be coupled with CPR training efforts. Such an ultimate coronary care unit may then include the following: 1) the ability of many laypersons in the community to recognize symptoms of possible myocardial infarction and to develop mechanisms to assure the victim of suspected myocardial infarction the benefits of timely monitoring and treatment, 2) broad capability among laypersons to support the life of the cardiac arrest victim until ACLS becomes available, 3) a mechanism for the recognition of persons at high risk for myocardial infarction and sudden cardiac death by virtue of established diagnosis of CHD, so that effective control programs (secondary prevention) might then be implemented, and 4) recognition, reduction, and control of risk factors for CAD in persons free of clinical manifestations of CAD, especially the young (primary prevention).

Efforts to accomplish these goals are already under way in many areas. Scientific knowledge of the cause of CAD and the mechanisms of sudden cardiac death has greatly increased in recent years. Encouraging evidence suggests that mass media educational campaigns directed at an entire community may be effective in reducing the risk of cardiovascular disease.[70] CPR-ECC education is only a part of the strategy. It is now appropriate for the community to use its energy in parallel efforts for primary and secondary prevention of CHD.

Prevention of Cardiovascular Disease: A Proven Approach

Mortality from coronary heart disease, stroke, and other cardiovascular diseases (CVD) declined, respectively, 39%, 54%, and 19% between 1964 and 1984, contrasting with a decline of only 12% in mortality from noncardiovascular diseases.[1, 71] Among these declines, that of CHD mortality has had the greatest impact on overall life expectancy. Had the death rate due to CHD remained at the level observed in 1964, there would have been 400,000 more deaths due to CHD in 1984.

A number of factors have undoubtedly contributed to the decline in CVD mortality outlined above, i.e., improved approaches to CVD diagnosis and therapy, use of drugs that have a "cardio protective" effect on high-risk individuals, improved surgical techniques, improved ECC, and modification of CVD risk factors in the population.

The reduction of risk factors can reduce CVD mortality and morbidity, and successful intervention at a young age is the approach likely to have the greatest impact. At the same time, intervention later in life, e.g., middle age, cannot be ignored since prevention may slow the progression of arterial disease and can be expected to reduce mortality and morbidity as well. An understanding of the relation of individual risk factors to cardiovascular disease and an enthusiasm for modifying or eliminating risk factors remain the critical determinants in efforts to reduce cardiovascular morbidity and mortality.

Emergency Cardiac Care

Emergency cardiac care (ECC) includes all of the following elements: 1) recognizing early warning signs of heart attack, efforts to prevent complications, reassurance of the victim, and prompt availability of monitoring and treatment aspects of life support, 2) providing immediate BLS at the scene, when needed, 3) providing ACLS at the scene as quickly as possible to stabilize the victim before transportation, and 4) transferring the stabilized victim to an appropriate hospital where definitive medical care can be provided.

Emergency transportation alone, without life support, does not constitute ECC. Although transportation is an important aspect, the major emphasis of ECC is the stabilization of a victim of the life-threatening emergency.

Basic Life Support (BLS) and Advanced Cardiac Life Support (ACLS)

Within the definition of ECC, two important aspects — BLS and ACLS — need to be distinguished because the responsibility for making each aspect work rests with a different group, the strategy for developing each capability differs, and the execution of each involves a different population within the community.

Basic life support is that particular phase of ECC that either 1) prevents circulatory or respiratory arrest (or insufficiency) through prompt recognition and intervention, early entry into the EMS system, or both, or 2) externally supports the circulation and respiration of a victim of cardiac or respiratory arrest through CPR.[72] BLS can and should be initiated by any person present when cardiac or respiratory arrest occurs. The most important link in the CPR-ECC system in the community is the layperson. The BLS aspect of ECC is dependent for its success on the layperson's willingness to initiate CPR promptly and his or her ability to provide it effectively. Accordingly, responsibility for providing lifesaving BLS at this level can be considered primarily a public, community responsibility. It is the responsibility of the medical community, however, to educate the public to this responsibility and to provide support for community education and training. BLS also includes the teaching of risk factors and prevention through "prudent heart living" (see Chapter 2).

Advanced cardiac life support includes BLS plus the use of adjunctive equipment, the establishment of an intravenous line, the administration of fluids and drugs, cardiac monitoring, defibrillation, the control of arrhythmias, and postresuscitation care. It also includes establishing the communications necessary to ensure continuing care. Advanced cardiac life support requires the supervision of a physician in person at the scene, directing activities remotely, or directing activities by some other mechanism previously defined by the physician — such as standing orders.

To be effective, ECC should be an integral part of a community-wide emergency medical services (EMS) system. The system should be based on local community needs in terms of patient care and available resources and should be consistent with regional, state, and national guidelines. There is little question that EMS systems have had a positive impact on mortality and morbidity from out-of-hospital cardiac arrests.

Education and Communication

Components such as public education, professional education, and emergency medical communication are essential parts of the total emergency system.

The greatest risk of death from heart attack is in the first two hours after the onset of symptoms.[61, 64] Laypersons, particularly those recognized to be at high risk, must first be educated to recognize the usual manifestations of heart attack. They then must know how to gain access to the EMS system. The fastest way for an emergency medical team to respond is through the use of a universal emergency telephone number, such as 911. Once this number is established, it must be promoted through an educational program so that it will be identified in the minds of as many as possible within the community as the mechanism for immediate access to emergency care. If 911 is not available, education should include the appropriate local emergency number(s).

Each person should have a well-formulated plan of action for use in an emergency. This plan should be based on the best plan of action for the community. When symptoms suggest a heart attack, it is recommended that a mobile life support unit be summoned to reduce the elapsed time from the onset of symptoms to entry into an EMS system. In the absence of such a system, the victim should be taken without delay to an emergency department or other facility with 24-hour life support capability.

Teaching CPR

During the past 15 years a significant portion of the adult population of the United States has been trained in the techniques of CPR. In some areas more than one third of the adult nonmedical population has some information or training in CPR. However, in the majority of cases CPR has been initiated by healthcare providers and not by lay individuals. In addition, only a minority of physicians have become involved in delivering CPR/ACLS. Educational methods must be developed that will enhance the use of emergency rescue skills by both laypersons and healthcare providers and, thus, improve the outcome of cardiac emergencies.

There are many reasons why lay individuals do not become involved in performing CPR: lack of motivation, fear of doing harm, inability to remember exact sequences, and poor retention of psychomotor skills. Thus, a major goal is for laypersons to learn and retain information concerning CPR and to be sufficiently motivated to become involved. In an effort to enhance learning, several changes in education should be instituted.

A particular area of concern is the selection of students. Usually, the majority of lay individuals taking CPR are young adults who are not often exposed to high-risk individuals. An emphasis must be placed on the need to train families, neighbors, and co-workers of high-risk individuals. Guidelines to assist CPR-teaching organizations in identifying these groups should be developed. Modular courses should be used increasingly, making it possible for students to concentrate on that particular aspect of BLS most applicable to their situation. For example, the families of patients with heart disease could be taught one-rescuer CPR for adults, whereas young parents might wish to take a course in which only infant resuscitation is taught.

Emphasis should be placed on teaching one-rescuer CPR to laypersons. Two-rescuer CPR is seldom, if ever, used by lay rescuers — when help is summoned it most often comes in the form of EMS personnel, who then relieve the lay rescuer. Teaching the additional sequences and skills of two-rescuer CPR adds complexity, likely leading to decreased retention of the main techniques of single-rescuer CPR.

Role of the American Heart Association

The American Heart Association is a nonprofit voluntary health agency supported solely by private contributors, not government tax dollars, whose mission is "to reduce disability and death from cardiovascular diseases and stroke." It does so by supporting research, professional and public education, and community service programs.

Scientists supported by AHA research programs seek to understand the different forms of cardiovascular diseases. Scientific councils of the AHA look for ways to improve patient care and treatment. Education and community service programs of the AHA promote a healthful lifestyle for Americans.

Emergency cardiac care will continue to be a responsibility of the AHA as long as sudden cardiac death continues to be a problem. Emergency cardiac care should be interpreted as including the three accepted areas of AHA programs:

1. Public education
2. Professional education
3. Community programs

The role of the AHA in ECC was defined by the 1973 and 1979 conferences and modified by the 1985 conference.[46, 50, 51] The charges outlined in the 1986 *JAMA* supplement can be summarized as follows:

1. Establish and revise standards, and develop and distribute materials.
2. Develop community resources for training, and act as a catalyst in the community to develop a stratified emergency medical services system.
3. Direct professional and public education efforts.

Since the AHA has both the expertise and community involvement to effectively evaluate such programs, it must continue to bear the ultimate responsibility for monitoring and evaluating teaching and performance standards in ECC.

In 1963 the AHA established the Subcommittee on Cardiopulmonary Resuscitation. This was expanded in 1971 to the Subcommittee on Cardiopulmonary Resuscitation and Emergency Cardiac Care and subsequently renamed the Committee on Emergency Cardiac Care.

The American Heart Association Training Network

The training network, represented by a pyramid structure (Figure 1), provides a systematic mechanism for long-range strategic planning and training in BLS. It offers a means of involving more people in the program in an orderly way, which more equitably distributes the work load. The responsibilities of faculty members and instructors are discussed below. Information on appointment criteria, successful course completion, renewal, and reciprocity is presented in Chapter 16.

AHA Training Network

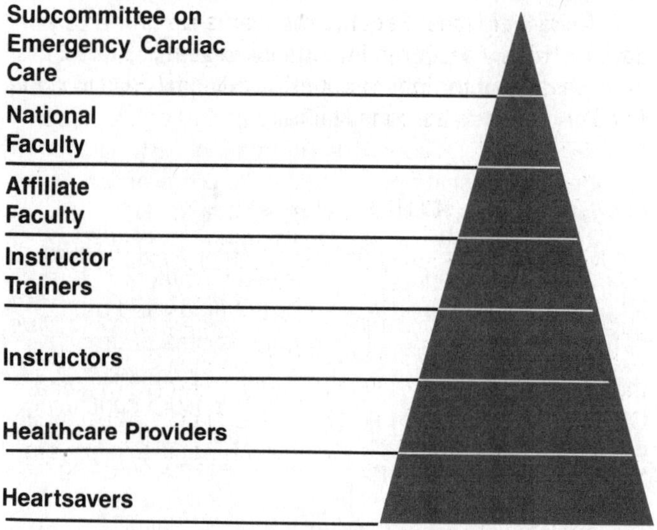

Subcommittee on Emergency Cardiac Care

National Faculty

Affiliate Faculty

Instructor Trainers

Instructors

Healthcare Providers

Heartsavers

Figure 1. Structure of the AHA training network pyramid.

National Faculty

The National Faculty consists of Instructors in BLS who have been appointed by the Committee on Emergency Cardiac Care to assist in the implementation of the training network. Such appointment is valid for two years and is reviewed biennially.

The National Faculty member may serve as a special consultant to the Committee on Emergency Cardiac Care and/or as a liaison between the Committee and the affiliates. A National Faculty member must work with the affiliate and should be intimately involved as a member and/or consultant of the affiliate/component Committee on Emergency Cardiac Care. One of their responsibilities is to disseminate information through the affiliate network. The National Faculty position may also be used for those who will implement the training network within the military (both inside and outside the United States).

The responsibilities of the National Faculty may include, but are not limited to, the following:

1. Organizing and implementing national training programs for Affiliate Faculty when the need is present
2. Assisting affiliates in the organization and implementation of training programs for Affiliate Faculty and Instructor Trainers in BLS
3. Assisting Affiliate Faculty in training Instructors in BLS
4. Assisting Instructors in training Providers in BLS
5. Consulting with the AHA Committee on Emergency Cardiac Care and assisting with special projects and programs as requested
6. Becoming involved in the development and implementation of local, state, or national EMS systems
7. Assisting the affiliate/component committee responsible for planning, implementing, and evaluating their ECC programs
8. Guiding and assisting medical training institutions in integrating BLS courses into the curriculum

One BLS National Faculty member is nominated by each affiliate. The Committee on Emergency Cardiac Care reserves the right to appoint additional BLS National Faculty members as consultants.

Associate Faculty

The Associate Faculty consists of Instructors in BLS and ACLS outside of the United States who have been appointed by the Committee on Emergency Cardiac Care to assist in the implementation of the training network in their home country. This designation in the international CPR program is the equivalent of the National Faculty in the training network of the AHA. Such appointments are valid for two years.

Associate Faculty members serve as liaisons from their countries to the Committee on Emergency Cardiac Care and are responsible for organizing the training network in their respective countries.

The responsibilities of the Associate Faculty may also include, but are not limited to, the following:

1. Organizing and coordinating the training program in CPR in their country
2. Training Instructors in BLS and ACLS
3. Consulting with the AHA Committee on Emergency Cardiac Care on CPR programs or other special projects
4. Becoming involved in the development and implementation of EMS systems within their own countries
5. Assisting the AHA in the renewal of training of individuals in that country who successfully completed courses in the United States
6. Assisting the AHA in the translation of teaching material from English to the local language
7. Preparing an annual report to the AHA National Center, including the number of BLS and ACLS courses given in the country and the number of individuals trained at different levels (Provider, Instructor, etc.)

Affiliate Faculty

The Affiliate Faculty consists of Instructors in BLS who have been appointed by the *affiliate committee* responsible for ECC. The affiliate committee may require attendance at an Affiliate Faculty workshop prior to appointment or reappointment. Such an appointment is valid *only* within that affiliate and is made on a yearly basis. The Affiliate Faculty is responsible for the implementation of the training network within the affiliate and, hence, should consist of experienced Instructors who are actively involved in teaching BLS.

The responsibilities of the Affiliate Faculty may include, but are not limited to, the following:

1. Training Instructors
2. Monitoring Instructors for successful course completion and renewal
3. Assisting the affiliate committee whose responsibility it is to plan, implement, and evaluate ECC programs
4. Becoming involved in the development and implementation of local and state emergency medical service systems
5. Guiding and assisting training institutions in integrating BLS into the curriculum

The Instructor

An Instructor is one who has successfully completed the AHA Instructor Course in BLS and who has received a satisfactory monitor's report while serving as an Instructor in a subsequent course. BLS Instructors must keep their BLS Provider status current during their tenure as a BLS Instructor. *Successful course completion at the Instructor level should be acknowledged by all affiliates and should not be limited to any geographic area.* For Instructors moving from one area to another, a period of orientation to local policies and procedures may be required. Successful course completion as an Instructor is valid for two years. The responsibilities of an Instructor are as follows:

1. Train Providers to successfully complete course. The Instructor may serve as Course Director in a BLS Provider Course
2. Serve, if needed and appointed, as a faculty member in a BLS Instructor Course
3. Assist the committee responsible to plan, implement, and evaluate its ECC program

The Instructor Trainer

Instructor Trainers are Instructors in BLS who have been appointed by the affiliate/component committee responsible for ECC. The appointing committee may require attendance at an Instructor Trainer workshop prior to appointment or reappointment. Such an appointment is valid only within the jurisdiction of the appointing committee and is made on a yearly basis. "Instructor Trainer" designates experienced Instructors who will be responsible for implementing the training network within the affiliate and/or component. They should assist the Affiliate Faculty, or assume their responsibilities completely when no Affiliate Faculty is available. *The designation of Instructor Trainers is optional* and is made principally by affiliates and their components when sufficient Affiliate Faculty members are not available.

The responsibilities of an Instructor Trainer are to

1. Train Instructors (they may serve as Course Directors in BLS Instructor or Provider courses)
2. Monitor Instructors for the purpose of successful course completion and renewal
3. Assist the AHA component committee whose responsibility it is to plan, implement, and evaluate ECC programs
4. Become involved in the development and implementation of local and state EMS systems
5. Guide and assist training institutions in integrating BLS into the curriculum

The Provider

A BLS Provider is one who has successfully completed the written examination and all performance (skills) testing of an AHA BLS Provider Course according to AHA requirements. Attendance at the lecture and practice sessions, although highly recommended, is not required. Successful completion at the provider level should be recognized by all affiliates and should not be limited to any geographic area. Course completion is valid for a maximum of two years. However, Providers should be encouraged to have at least annual renewal sessions to minimize the loss of psychomotor skills. Individual states, communities, hospitals, or organizations may have more stringent requirements for renewal of training for individual Providers to meet specific local needs.

CPR Training Systems

Public Education and Community Programs Target Sites

Public education and community programs are designed and developed for the individual, the family, and the community. Public education and community programs are priority health interventions, methods, or activities that are based on compelling or conclusive scientific evidence and that may also have a health or treatment benefit. They are developed, field tested, and packaged in modular form for use by affiliates. A module includes guidelines for implementation, marketing, and evaluation. Educational materials and audiovisuals are prepackaged for affiliate use. Community programs are designed to modify or change individual and/or community attitudes and practices to improve cardiovascular health and decrease morbidity and mortality from disease of the heart and blood vessels. To reach the public with authoritative information on cardiovascular health, the AHA Program Committee has selected four specific sites within the community where impact can be the greatest (referred to as target sites) — the schoolsite, the worksite,

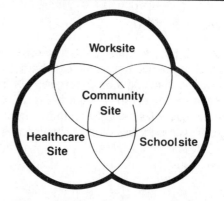

Figure 2. The interrelationship of the schoolsite, the worksite, the healthcare site, and the community site.

the healthcare site, and the community site (Figure 2). These locations offer controlled settings that can provide established networks of communication, staff for the delivery of messages or services, and independent funding mechanisms to carry out programs. The target sites further provide the ideal setting for followup and evaluation.

The ECC program package contains specific course materials, the ECC standards, and program management guidelines. Because public education in CPR is required if the AHA is to achieve its goal of reducing disability and death from cardiovascular diseases and stroke, BLS training is an essential part of community education.

It is the responsibility of the AHA to develop, maintain, and distribute the standards for emergency cardiac care. It is also the role of the AHA to assist the community in developing educational programs, to make them self-supporting where possible, and to perpetuate the skills of CPR.

Mass Training

Mass training[73] may be one answer to the growing demand for CPR. The notion of training large numbers of people in one day or one weekend is not new, but its practice on a national scale is limited. One of the original mass training programs was Project Lifesaver in the Greater Kansas City area. In 1980, 2,000 people were trained in one day in the Royals Stadium. In 1981, 13,400 people were similarly trained in a Mother's Day event. Equally impressive has been Project CPR, sponsored by the North Central Texas Council of Governments and local chapters of the American Heart Association/American Red Cross (ARC), in which 13,800 people were trained in a single weekend.

In the summer of 1981 the National Broadcasting Corporation (NBC) and the ARC conducted a national television CPR program coincident with an increased availability of CPR training in all ARC chapters. The program did not meet anticipated goals as a mass training program; however, it did create significant long-term increases in CPR class enrollments. The effort was repeated in 1982 with greater success. The NBC-ARC program and other mass training efforts such as the Texas Project CPR introduced the concept of media CPR. With increased use of television, mass training should also increase.

Hundreds of mass training events developed across the country have been successful as a result of adequate planning. Mass training procedures have been refined and programs are easier to conduct. General suggestions from previous sessions are presented for those Instructors who may wish to undertake mass training projects.

1. Preregistration is a must in planning for instructors and manikins. Course over-enrollment is good planning and should be encouraged. In Project Lifesaver the dropout rate was 30%.
2. Phone registration is usually more efficient than mail registration.
3. A central control center should be established for each training site. Responsibilities of the center include the number of instructors needed; the number of students who regist, attend, and successfully complete the course; and maintenance of manikins.
4. The number of training sites should be kept to a minimum. It is easier to monitor a few large sites than many small sites. Schools, field houses, gymnasiums, and cafeterias that can accommodate up to 200 people make ideal settings for mass training. While hospitals often supply many instructors, training at hospitals is often limited to small rooms, which is a disadvantage.
5. Sites should be available at all hours on each day the mass training is planned.
6. The subject matter portion of the course should be presented by television or videotape rather than lectures. This approach provides efficiency, consistency, and effectiveness in the short time available.
7. There must be uniformity in instruction and coordination for instructors. While national standards for CPR exist, instructors are subject to their own interpretations of the standards. With instructors from a variety of backgrounds, the situation is ripe for conflict. Conflict in concepts is a source of confusion for the student and will detract from the understanding and ability to perform CPR. All information must be compatible. Instructor orientation before the program is a necessity. Since instructor dropout can be anticipated, substitutes should be recruited.
8. Long waiting lines for manikin practice and testing can detract from the overall effectiveness of a program and may turn people away. Contributing causes may be poor allocation of equipment, insufficient equipment, too few instructors, poor design of practice and testing stations, and underestimation of the potential number of students in the program. Good planning can reduce the incidence of problems.
9. If a repair service is not available at each site, a roving repair service should be available for dispatching from a central center.
10. Records of students successfully completing the course should be maintained for future contact about renewal courses.

The Interactive CPR Learning System

In 1980 the AHA National Center and the Committee on Emergency Cardiac Care began the design of an interactive videodisc system for teaching BLS. This CPR Learning System was originally developed by the AHA as a means of significantly increasing the number of persons trained in CPR by providing a standardized course of high quality not requiring an increased number of instructors. This challenge was achieved through a blending of recent technological advances and an innovative learning theory that permits the CPR student to learn from the "victim" rather than an instructor.

It was understood that the new system must be consistent with the high standards for training that existed throughout the training network and affiliate structure. A further objective was to provide a standardized method for BLS teaching and training, as provided from the Committee on Emergency Cardiac Care.

By late 1982 a prototype system confirmed that an instructorless CPR training system was possible. The AHA obtained a patent on the system and sought a company to complete development and distribution. Actronics, Inc., was chosen after agreeing to 1) repay the AHA for all development costs, 2) provide royalties to the AHA on each sale, and 3) give total control of program content to the Committee on Emergency Cardiac Care.

In 1983 the CPR Learning System was introduced. It won two prestigious awards for the AHA, and validation studies confirmed its ability to train and test individuals in CPR competence.[74]

The technology of the CPR system includes a microcomputer interfaced with a videodisc player, an interactive audiocassette player, and a CPR manikin wired with a series of electronic sensors. The learning theory presumes that student performance can be improved by immediate feedback. Performance can be repeated until correct.

The entire CPR course is presented in this self-contained, stand-alone system, but because of its interactive nature, the system actually tailors the content of the course to respond to each student's individual needs. Like the traditional method of teaching CPR, the program consists of stimulating lectures, manikin training and testing, and a complete BLS course completion performance test at the end.

During the lectures the computer evaluates student progress through multiple-choice or fill-in-the-blank questions. Based on this evaluation, appropriate material is selected by the computer for review or more in-depth instruction. At any point the student can stop the program (restarting from that point at a later time), take a break, review specific material, request to be tested, practice on the manikin, or access a vocabulary bank (which defines a number of concepts by presenting technical information on three different levels of detail).

Adult and infant manikins, wired with electronic sensors to monitor the depth and placement of cardiac compressions, interface with the computer. In addition, the adult manikin monitors the adequacy of mouth-to-mouth ventilations and subdiaphragmatic abdominal thrusts (the Heimlich maneuver). The system provides four different types of feedback: 1) audiovisual coaching, 2) visual display on the computer monitor (indicating, for example, that hand placement is incorrect or depth of compression is too shallow), 3) audio tones to indicate the proper timing of each compression, and 4) a graphic summary on the computer monitor that details overall performance. The student receives this feedback almost simultaneously as the computer accesses the appropriate comments in response to each compression or set of compressions.

Since the CPR system is considered an extension of the training network, a national AHA-CPR course completion card is issued by the system to acknowledge that the student has met the standards of CPR performance as set by the national AHA Committee on Emergency Cardiac Care. The CPR card is valid for not more than two years, and retraining on a learning system is recommended annually.

A CPR renewal system has been developed to provide the same high testing standards as the CPR Learning System. This additional system, intended to be used as an instructor's aid, provides the same objective evaluation and performance skills in both practice and testing modes as the CPR Learning System, but without audio and video support. It can be supplemented with instructor-presented educational materials to provide the high-quality training experience of the original CPR Learning System.

Summary

Cardiovascular diseases claim almost as many American lives as all other causes of death combined. This chapter has summarized the efforts of medical and lay communities to bring together knowledge and expertise to address this significant problem. Emergency cardiac care encompasses basic life support, advanced cardiac life support, education, communications, and transport. The American Heart Association provides support for control of cardiovascular disease through research, education, and community service programs. The AHA training network is a structure for education that also incorporates quality control.

References

1. *1987 Heart Facts.* Dallas, American Heart Association, 1986, pp 2–7.
2. Eisenberg MS, Bergner L, Hallstrom A: Cardiac resuscitation in the community: Importance of rapid provision and implications for program planning. *JAMA* 1979;241:1905–1907.
3. Lund I, Skulberg A: Cardiopulmonary resuscitation by lay people. *Lancet* 1976;2:702–704.
4. Carveth S: Eight year experience with a stadium-based mobile coronary care unit. *Heart Lung* 1974;3:770–774.
5. Thompson RG, Hallstrom AP, Cobb LA: Bystander-initiated cardiopulmonary resuscitation in the management of ventricular fibrillation. *Ann Intern Med* 1979;90:737–740.
6. Kouwenhoven WB, Jude JR, Knickerbocker GG: Closed-chest cardiac massage. *JAMA* 1960;173:1064–1067.
7. Cardiopulmonary resuscitation: Statement by the Ad Hoc Committee on Cardiopulmonary Resuscitation of the Division of Medical Sciences, National Academy of Sciences–National Research Council. *JAMA* 1966; 198:372–379.
8. *Cardiopulmonary Resuscitation: Conference Proceedings, May 23, 1966.* Washington, DC, National Academy of Sciences–National Research Council, 1967.
9. *Emergency Resuscitation Team Manual: A Hospital Plan.* New York, American Heart Association, 1968.
10. *Emergency Measures in Cardiopulmonary Resuscitation.* New York, American Heart Association, 1971.
11. *Definitive Therapy in Cardiopulmonary Resuscitation.* New York, American Heart Association, 1971.
12. *Cardiopulmonary Resuscitation: A Manual for Instructors.* New York, American Heart Association, 1971.
13. *Training of Ambulance Personnel in Cardiopulmonary Resuscitation.* New York, American Heart Association, 1965.
14. *The Dentist's Role in Cardiopulmonary Resuscitation.* New York, American Heart Association, 1968.
15. *Training of Lifeguards in Cardiopulmonary Resuscitation.* New York, American Heart Association, 1970.
16. *Accidental Death and Disability: The Neglected Disease of Modern Society.* Committee on Trauma and Committee on Shock, Division of Medical Sciences. Washington, DC, National Academy of Sciences–National Research Council, 1966.
17. *Medical Requirements for Ambulance Design and Equipment,* bulletin 8774. Committee on Emergency Medical Services, Division of Medical Sciences. Washington, DC, National Academy of Sciences–National Research Council, 1970.
18. *Ambulance Design Criteria,* bulletin 6032. Committee on Ambulance Design Criteria of the Highway Research Board, Division of Engineering. Washington, DC, National Academy of Sciences–National Research Council, June 1969.
19. *Training of Ambulance Personnel and Others Responsible for Emergency Care of the Sick and Injured at the Scene and During Transport,* bulletin 8775. Committee on Emergency Medical Services, Division of Medical Sciences. Washington, DC, National Academy of Sciences–National Research Council:, 1970.
20. *Refresher Training Program for Emergency Medical Technician — Ambulance,* course guide, bulletin 9984. Washington, DC, U.S. Department of Transportation, National Highway Traffic Safety Administration, 1971.
21. *Roles and Resources of Federal Agencies in Support of Comprehensive Emergency Medical Services,* bulletin 25269. Washington, DC, U.S. Department of Health, Education, and Welfare, National Academy of Sciences–National Research Council, 1972.
22. Wright IS, Fredrickson DT: Cardiovascular disease-acute care: Introduction: Inter-relationship among health facilities: Future role of modern communication and transportation; electronic equipment in critical care areas: Status of devices currently in use; resources for the optimal acute care of patients with congenital heart disease. Report of Inter-Society Commission for Heart Disease Resources, abstracted. *Circulation* 1971;43:97–99, 101–133.
23. Cardiovascular disease — acute care: Resources for the management of emergencies in hypertension. Report of Inter-Society Commission for Heart Disease Resources, abstracted. *Circulation* 1971;43:157–160.
24. Cardiovascular disease — acute care: Resources for the acute care of peripheral vascular diseases. Report of Inter-Society Commission for Heart Disease Resources, abstracted. *Circulation* 1971;43:161–169.
25. Cardiovascular disease — acute care: Resources for the optimal care of patients with acute myocardial infarction. Report of Inter-Society Commission for Heart Disease Resources, abstracted. *Circulation* 1971; 43:171–183.
26. Cardiovascular disease — acute care: Resources for the optimal care of acute respiratory failure. Report of Inter-Society Commission for Heart Disease Resources, abstracted. *Circulation* 1971;43:185–195.
27. Cardiovascular disease — electronic equipment in critical care areas Part II: The electrical environment. Report by the Instrumentation Study Group of the Inter-Society Commission for Heart Disease Resources, abstracted. *Circulation* 1971;44::237–246.
28. Critical performance criteria — defibrillators, report by the Instrumentation Study Group of the Inter-Society Commission for Heart Disease Resources, abstracted. *Circulation* 1973;47:359–361.
29. *Basic Training Program for Emergency Medical Technician — Ambulance: Concepts and Recommendations,* bulletin 7802. U.S. Department of Transportation, National Highway Safety Bureau, 1970.
30. *Basic Training Program for Emergency Medical Technician — Ambulance: Instructor's Lesson Plans,* bulletin 14958. U.S. Department of Transportation, National Highway Safety Bureau, 1970.
31. *Communications — Guidelines for Emergency Medical Services.* U.S. Department of Transportation, National Highway Traffic Safety Administration, 1972.
32. *Emergency Medical Services Communications Systems,* bulletin 20369. U.S. Department of Health, Education, and Welfare, Health Services and Mental Health Administration, 1972.
33. *Compendium of State Statutes on the Regulation of Ambulance Services, Operation of Emergency Vehicles, and Good Samaritan Laws,* bulletin 13341. Health Services and Mental Health Administration, Division of Emergency Health Services, 1969.
34. *Emergency Health Services Selected Bibliography.* Health Services and Mental Health Administration, Division of Emergency Health Services, 1970.
35. Essential equipment for ambulances, American College of Surgeons Committee on Trauma. *Bull Am Coll Surg* 1970;55:7–13.
36. *Emergency Care and Transportation of the Sick and Injured,* ed 3. American Academy of Orthopedic Surgeons. Chicago, American Academy of Orthopedic Surgeons, 1971.
37. *Developing Emergency Medical Services: Guidelines for Community Councils,* American Medical Association Commission of Emergency Medical Services. Chicago, American Medical Association, 1973.
38. Community-wide emergency medical services: Recommendations by the Committee on Acute Medicine of the American Society of Anesthesiologists. *JAMA* 1968;204:595–602.
39. Safar P: *Cardiopulmonary Resuscitation: A Manual for Physicians and Paramedical Instructors.* Pittsburgh, World Federation Society of Anesthesiologists, 1968.
40. Manually-operated resuscitators. *Health Devices* 1971;1:13–17.
41. Inspection of defibrillators. *Health Devices* 1971;1:109–113.
42. Battery-operated defibrillators/monitors. *Health Devices* 1973;2:87103.
43. Line-operated synchronized defibrillators. *Health Devices* 1973;2:117–129.
44. External cardiac compressors. *Health Devices* 1973;2:136–151.
45. Yu PN: Prehospital care of acute myocardial infarction. *Circulation* 1972;45:189–204.
46. Standards for Cardiopulmonary Resuscitation (CPR) and Emergency Cardiac Care (ECC). *JAMA* 1974;227(suppl): 796, 797, 833–868.
47. *CPR Lifesaving Techniques.* Gallup Poll, Princeton, NJ, June 1977.
48. *Proceedings of the First National Conference on the Medicolegal Implications of Emergency Medical Care.* Dallas, American Heart Association, 1976.
49. *Report on Emergency Airway Management.* Committee on Emergency Medical Services, Assembly of Life Sciences, National Research Council, National Academy of Sciences, 1976.
50. Standards and Guidelines for Cardiopulmonary Resuscitation (CPR) and Emergency Cardiac Care (ECC). *JAMA* 1980;244(suppl)453–509.

51. Standards and Guidelines for Cardiopulmonary Resuscitation (CPR) and Emergency Cardiac Care (ECC). *JAMA* 1986;255:2905–2992.

52. Proceedings of the 1985 National Conference on Standards and Guidelines for Cardiopulmoinary Resuscitation and Emergency Cardiac Care. *Circulation* 1986;74(suppl IV):1–153.

53. Carveth SW, Burnap TK, Bechtel J, et al: Training in advanced cardiac life support: *JAMA* 1976;235:2311–2315.

54. *Heart Facts 1984.* Dallas, American Heart Association, 1983, p 2.

55. Bainton CR, Peterson DR: Deaths from coronary heart disease in persons 50 years of age and younger: A community-wide study. *N Engl J Med* 1963;268:569–575.

56. McNeilly RH, Pemberton J: Duration of last attack in 998 fatal cases of coronary artery disease and its relation to possible cardiac resuscitation. *Br Med J* 1968;3:139–142.

57. Kuller L, Lilienfeld A, Fisher R: Epidemiological study of sudden and unexpected deaths due to arteriosclerotic heart disease. *Circulation* 1966;34:1056–1068.

58. Gordon T, Kannel WB: Premature mortality from coronary heart disease: The Framingham study. *JAMA* 1971;215:1617–1625.

59. Shu CY: Mobile CCUs. *Hospitals* 1971;45:14.

60. Kuller L, Cooper M, Perper J, et al: Epidemiology of sudden death. *Arch Intern Med* 1972;129:714.

61. Kuller L, Lilienfeld A, Fisher R: Sudden and unexpected deaths in young adults: An epidemiological study. *JAMA* 1966;198:248–252.

62. Pantridge JF, Geddes JS: Cardiac arrest after myocardial infarction. *Lancet* 1966;1:807–808.

63. Grace WJ, Chadbourn JA: The mobile coronary care unit. *Dis Chest* 1969;55:452–455.

64. Pantridge JF: The effect of early therapy on the hospital mortality from acute myocardial infarction. *Q J Med* 1970;39:621–622.

65. Grace WJ, Chadbourn JA: The first hour in acute myocardial infarction. *Heart Lung* 1974;3:736–741.

66. Copley DP, Mantle JA, Rogers WJ, et al: Improved outcome from pre-hospital cardiopulmonary collapse with resuscitation by bystanders. *Circulation* 1977;56:901–905.

67. Gallup G: Campaign to educate Americans in CPR successful. Baton Rouge, La, *Sunday Advocate*, Nov. 27, 1983.

68. Gordon T, Kannel WB, McGee D, et al: Death and coronary attacks in men after giving up cigarette smoking: A report from the Framingham study. *Lancet* 1974;2:1345–1348.

69. Wilhelmeson G, Vedin JA, Elmfeldt D, et al: Smoking and myocardial infarction. *Lancet* 1975;1:415–420.

70. Farquhar JW, Maccoby N, Wood PD, et al: Community education for cardiovascular health. *Lancet* 1977;1:1192–1195.

71. National Center for Heart Statistics: Advance report of final mortality statistics, 1982. *Monthly Vital Statistics Rep* 1984;33(suppl):1–43.

72. *A Manual for Instructors of Basic Cardiac Life Support.* Dallas, American Heart Association, 1977.

73. Smith BH, Newman MJ: *The CPR Bluebook: A Program Management Guide.* ACT Foundation, 1982, pp 63–66.

74. Kaye W, Montgomery W, Hon D et al: Interactive computer-videodisc CPR training and testing (abstract). *Circulation* 1983;68(part II:suppl III):III–14.

Chapter 2

Cardiopulmonary Physiology, Dysfunction, and Actions for Survival

Information in this chapter includes the anatomy and physiology of the cardiovascular and respiratory systems, disease syndromes, prevention guidelines, and actions for survival. It explains when and why CPR becomes necessary.

The Cardiovascular and Respiratory Systems

Anatomy of the Cardiovascular System

The cardiovascular system is composed of the heart, arteries, capillaries, and veins. The heart of an adult is not much larger than a fist. It lies in the center of the chest, behind the breastbone (sternum), in front of the backbone (thoracic spine), and above the diaphragm. Except for the area of the heart against the spine and a small strip down the center of the front of the heart, it is surrounded by lung (Figure 3).

The heart is a hollow organ. Its tough, muscular wall (myocardium) is surrounded by a sac (pericardium) and has a thin, strong lining (endocardium). A wall (septum) divides the heart cavity into "right" and "left" sides of the heart. Each side is divided again into upper chamber (atrium) and lower chamber (ventricle). Valves regulate the flow of blood through the heart chambers and 1) into the pulmonary artery and then to the lungs or 2) into the aorta and then to the rest of the body (Figure 4).

Arteries, which have thick walls, carry blood under high pressure away from the heart. Arteries deliver blood to small capillaries that have walls only one cell thick. The capillaries eventually join together to form thin-walled veins that carry blood under low pressure back to the heart. The coronary arteries, which arise from the root of the aorta, supply the heart muscle with blood.

Physiology of the Heart

The function of the heart is to pump blood to the body and to the lungs. Arteries and veins carry the blood to and from the capillaries and the heart. It is at the capillary level that exchange of oxygen and carbon dioxide takes place between the blood and the tissues. This process occurs in the lungs, the rest of the body, and the heart muscle itself.

Oxygen is continually required by all body cells to carry out normal functions. Carbon dioxide is produced as a waste product and must be eliminated from the body through the lungs.

The heart is really a double pump. One pump (the right side of the heart) receives blood that has just come from the body after delivering oxygen to the body tissues. It pumps this dark, bluish-red blood to the lungs where the blood rids itself of waste gas (carbon dioxide) and picks

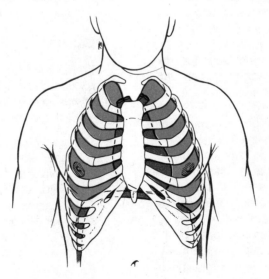

Figure 3. The heart in relation to other components of the chest.

The Heart and How It Works

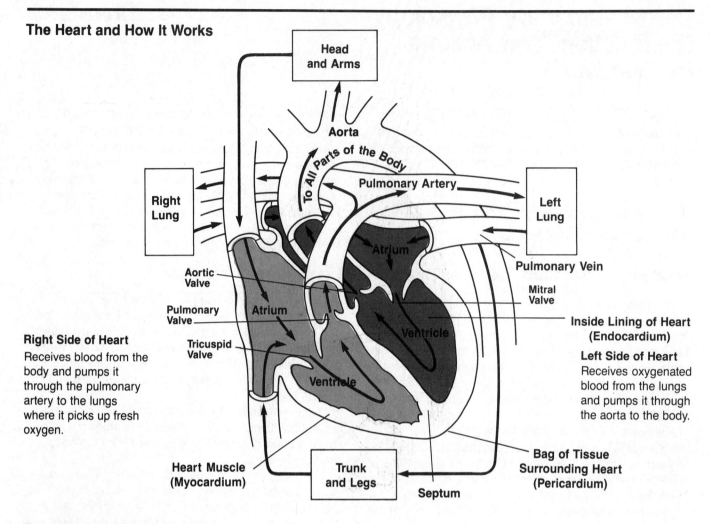

Right Side of Heart
Receives blood from the body and pumps it through the pulmonary artery to the lungs where it picks up fresh oxygen.

Left Side of Heart
Receives oxygenated blood from the lungs and pumps it through the aorta to the body.

Figure 4. Anatomy of the heart.

up a fresh supply of oxygen that turns it a bright red again. The second pump (the left side of the heart) forces blood through the great trunk artery (aorta) to be distributed by smaller arteries to all parts of the body.

The adult heart at rest pumps 60–100 times a minute, or approximately 100,000 times each day. Each time the adult heart beats, it ejects about 2½ ounces of blood (approximately 70 milliliters); therefore, the heart pumps about 5 quarts (approximately 5 liters) of blood each minute. During exercise the heart can pump up to 37 quarts (35 liters) each minute. The total blood volume of a 150-pound man is approximately 6 quarts (approximately 6 liters).

Each cardiac muscle contraction or heartbeat is preceded and initiated by an electrical impulse that arises from the natural pacemaker in the heart and is transmitted to the heart muscle by a specialized conduction system. The heart muscle contracts after it is stimulated by this electrical impulse. The contraction is followed by a period during which the electrical system and the heart muscle are recharged and made ready for the next beat. The heart has its own electrical pacemaker. Even if the heart is removed from the body, it will continue to beat if

properly maintained. The heart rate, however, can be altered either by nervous impulses from the brain or by various substances in the blood that influence the pacemaker and the conduction system.

Anatomy of the Respiratory System

The respiratory system has four components: 1) an *airway* from the outside of the body to the inside, 2) a *neuromuscular system*, 3) the *alveoli*, and 4) the *arteries, capillaries,* and *veins* (Figure 5).

1. The airway is composed of the following elements:
   A. Upper Airway
      (1) Nose and mouth
      (2) Pharynx (behind the tongue)
      (3) Larynx or voice box
   B. Lower Airway
      (1) Trachea or windpipe
      (2) Bronchi, one to the right lung and one to the left lung
      (3) Bronchioles, branches of the bronchi that terminate in the alveoli

The Respiratory System

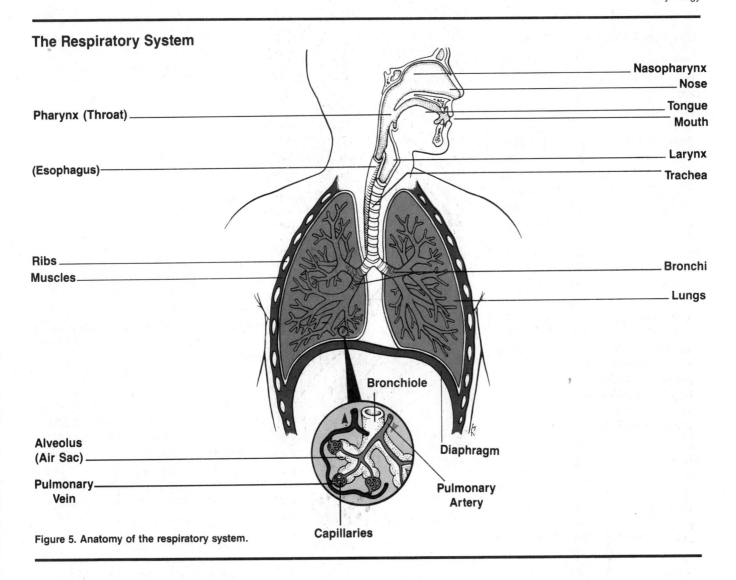

Nasopharynx
Nose
Tongue
Mouth
Larynx
Trachea
Pharynx (Throat)
(Esophagus)
Ribs
Muscles
Bronchi
Lungs
Bronchiole
Diaphragm
Alveolus (Air Sac)
Pulmonary Vein
Pulmonary Artery
Capillaries

Figure 5. Anatomy of the respiratory system.

2. The neuromuscular system is composed of the respiratory center in the brain, the nerves to the muscles of respiration, and the muscles of respiration. In addition, the chest cage, composed of the ribs supported in back by the spine and in front by the sternum, protects the lungs and allows breathing to occur. The major muscles of respiration are a) the large sheet-like diaphragm attached to the margin of the lower ribs, extending from front to back, and separating the chest cavity from the abdominal cavity; b) the muscles between the ribs (the intercostal muscles); and c) some of the muscles of the neck and shoulder girdle.

3. The alveoli, millions of tiny air sacs that contain carbon dioxide and oxygen, are lined by a membrane. There is a fine network of capillaries on the other side of the membrane. The alveoli, with their associated capillaries, are the basic lung unit.

4. The pulmonary arteries carry blood, with low oxygen content, from the heart; the capillaries surround the alveoli; and the pulmonary veins carry blood, with high oxygen content, back to the heart.

Physiology of Respiration

The function of the respiratory system is to bring oxygen from the outside air into the blood and to eliminate carbon dioxide. The cells of the body are continuously in need of oxygen to function, and as a result of using this oxygen, carbon dioxide is produced. Unless oxygen is continually supplied and carbon dioxide is continually eliminated from the body, death will result. The cardiovascular system transports oxygen from the lungs to the cells of the body and transports carbon dioxide from the cells to the lungs for elimination.

The stimulus to breathe comes from the respiratory center in the brain, but the prime stimulus for altering the depth and rate of breaths is the level of carbon dioxide in the arterial blood. As the level rises, the respiratory center in the brain sends an increasing number of signals by way of nerves to the muscles of respiration. The breathing rate and depth are increased until the level of carbon dioxide falls, and then the breathing rate slows. There is a continual feedback loop between the carbon dioxide level and the rate and depth of respiration.

At the level of the alveoli, oxygen from the air passes into the blood through the alveolar and capillary walls, and carbon dioxide passes in the opposite direction.

Atmospheric air contains about 21% oxygen and negligible amounts of carbon dioxide. During respiration only about a quarter of the oxygen in the inhaled air is taken up by the blood in the lungs so that exhaled air still contains significant oxygen (about 16%) as well as a small amount of added carbon dioxide (5%) and water vapor. In CPR, the exhaled air of rescue breaths contains enough oxygen to support the life of the victim.

Inspiration is an active process. As the intercostal muscles contract, they elevate the ribs upward and forward; as the diaphragm contracts, it descends toward the abdominal cavity. The lungs expand and the pressure within the lungs becomes less than that outside of the chest. Air moves into the airways and lungs. Expiration is generally a passive process. As the muscles relax, the ribs descend and the diaphragm rises, thereby decreasing the capacity of the chest cavity. The elastic lung passively becomes smaller, and the air inside the lung moves out.

Respiratory Arrest and Insufficiency

Respiratory arrest refers to the absence of breathing. (Respiratory failure implies that, although breathing may be present, it is inadequate to maintain normal levels of oxygen and carbon dioxide in the blood.)

Airway Obstruction

The obstructed airway is discussed in detail in Chapter 7. The most common cause of airway obstruction is the tongue and epiglottis. Any condition that leads to unconsciousness or loss of tone in the muscles of the jaw can cause the tongue to fall toward the back of the pharynx and obstruct the airway and the epiglottis to occlude the entrance to the larynx.[1]

Foreign body obstruction of the airway accounted for 3,100 deaths in 1984.[2] The need for proper emergency airway management in cases of foreign body obstruction is of key importance for safety in homes, restaurants, and other public places.

Central Respiratory Arrest

Since the respiratory center in the brain must function for respiration to occur, any condition that depresses or destroys the respiratory center will cause respiration to cease. A common cause is inadequate blood flow to the brain, as occurs in shock or cardiac arrest. Within a few seconds after the heart ceases to beat, respiration will cease. (This is in contrast to the heart's continuing to beat for several minutes after breathing ceases. In fact, any condition that leads to inadequate oxygenation of the blood, despite adequate blood flow to the brain, can lead

to respiratory arrest.) Other causes include stroke (a condition caused by interruption of the blood supply to an area of the brain, analogous to a myocardial infarction or heart attack that occurs when blood supply to an area of heart muscle is interrupted), drug overdose, use of narcotics and barbiturates, head trauma, and diseases or injuries that interfere with normal contraction of the muscles of respiration.

Coronary Artery Disease

Definition of Terms

Arteriosclerosis, commonly called "hardening of the arteries", includes a variety of conditions that cause the artery walls to thicken and lose elasticity.

Atherosclerosis is a form of arteriosclerosis in which the inner layers of artery walls become thick and irregular due to deposits of a fatty substance. As the interior walls of arteries become lined with layers of these deposits, the arteries become narrowed and the flow of blood through the arteries is reduced.

Coronary artery disease (CAD) is the presence of atherosclerosis in the coronary arteries.

Coronary heart disease (CHD) is coronary artery disease plus the presence of symptoms as manifested by angina (specific chest pain) or a history of acute myocardial infarction. The term *atherosclerotic heart disease* is synonymous with coronary heart disease.

Ischemic heart disease is a more general term that includes all causes of myocardial ischemia (poor oxygen supply to the heart muscle).

Pathology and Natural History

Atherosclerosis is a slow, progressive disease that may have its beginnings early in life. (Significant disease may be present before the age of 20. Long before the function of the heart muscle is impaired, there exists an asymptomatic period when risk factor modification may halt or reverse the process.) The inner portion of the arterial wall (especially the intima) becomes thickened with deposits of fats (lipid, cholesterol), fibrin, and eventually, calcium. The result is a gradual narrowing of the arterial lumen (Figure 6). When the blood flow is severely reduced by atherosclerosis, a clot can form as blood trickles and sludges through the narrowed vessel, causing a sudden, complete stoppage of blood flow. Injury to the heart muscle occurs because of this decrease or interruption of blood flow, creating an imbalance between the demand of the heart muscle for oxygen and the ability of the narrowed coronary artery to meet that demand.

Atherosclerosis is a generalized arterial disease that may involve arteries in different areas such as the heart (leading to a heart attack), the brain (leading to a stroke), or the legs (leading to intermittent claudication, i.e., pain precipitated by walking, or leg cramps during exercise).

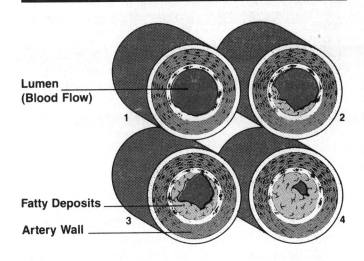

Lumen (Blood Flow)

Fatty Deposits

Artery Wall

Figure 6. Progressive atherosclerotic buildup on artery walls.

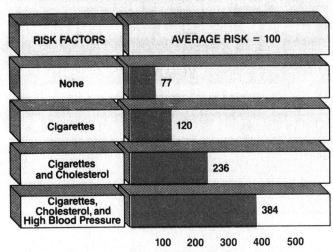

RISK FACTORS	AVERAGE RISK = 100
None	77
Cigarettes	120
Cigarettes and Cholesterol	236
Cigarettes, Cholesterol, and High Blood Pressure	384

100   200   300   400   500

Source: The Framingham, MA, Heart Study

Figure 7. The danger of heart attack increases with the number of risk factors present.[3] For purposes of illustration, this chart uses an abnormal blood pressure level of 180 systolic and a cholesterol level of 310 in a 45-year-old man.

Risk Factors

As investigators have searched for the causes of the "epidemic" of blood vessel diseases in this and many other countries, a consistent association has been found between specific conditions and behaviors and the development of blood vessel disease. The "risk factor" concept developed from an awareness of these associations.

It is now well known that heart attack occurs much more frequently in individuals who smoke cigarettes, have elevated blood cholesterol levels, and have elevated blood pressure. Evidence indicates that each of the risk factors increases the risk of heart attack or other blood vessel disease roughly in proportion to the degree of incidence or use. That is, the person who smokes one pack of cigarettes a day has a greater chance of heart attack and sudden death than a person who does not smoke, other things being equal. The person who smokes two packs of cigarettes a day, in turn, has a greater chance of heart attack and sudden death than the person who smokes one pack, and a much greater chance than the person who doesn't smoke cigarettes at all. The same is true of serum cholesterol and other risk factors.

Further, individuals who have more than one risk factor may have many more times the chance of developing vascular disease than individuals who have none. For example, the individual who has an abnormal serum cholesterol level and smokes two packs of cigarettes a day may have as much as 10 times the chance of having a heart attack as the person who has a normal blood cholesterol level and does not smoke. Figure 7 illustrates the incidence of the three major risk factors for coronary heart disease — cigarette smoking, elevated blood cholesterol, and elevated blood pressure — and their relation to the likelihood of heart attack.

Risk Factors That Cannot Be Changed

Some risk factors cannot be modified or eliminated (Figure 8).

Heredity: A history of premature CHD in siblings or parents suggests an increased susceptibility that may be a genetic factor.

Sex: Women have a lower incidence of coronary atherosclerosis prior to menopause. The incidence increases significantly in postmenopausal women.

Race: Black Americans have approximately a 45% greater chance of having high blood pressure (a contributor to heart attack and stroke) than whites.

Age: The death rate from CHD increases with age. However, nearly 1 in 4 deaths occur in persons under age 65.

Risk Factors That Can Be Changed

Other risk factors *are* subject to modification or elimination (Figure 8).

Cigarette Smoking: The heart attack death rate among people who do not smoke cigarettes is considerably lower than for people who do smoke. For those who have given up the habit, the death rate eventually declines almost to that of people who have never smoked.

High Blood Pressure: A major risk factor of stroke and heart attack, high blood pressure usually has no specific symptoms but can be detected by a simple, painless test. A person with mild elevations of blood pressure often begins treatment with a program of weight reduction, if overweight, and salt (sodium) restriction before drugs are recommended.

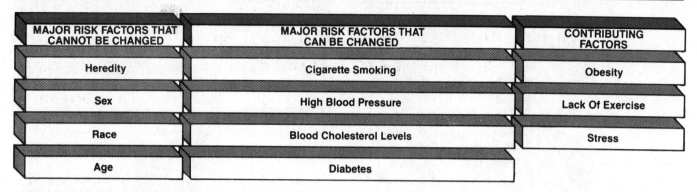

MAJOR RISK FACTORS THAT CANNOT BE CHANGED	MAJOR RISK FACTORS THAT CAN BE CHANGED	CONTRIBUTING FACTORS
Heredity	Cigarette Smoking	Obesity
Sex	High Blood Pressure	Lack Of Exercise
Race	Blood Cholesterol Levels	Stress
Age	Diabetes	

Figure 8. Risk factors of heart disease.

High Blood Cholesterol Levels: Too much cholesterol can cause buildups on the walls of arteries, narrowing the passageway through which blood flows and leading to heart attack and stroke. A doctor can measure the amount of cholesterol in the blood by a simple test. Since the body gets cholesterol both through diet and by manufacturing it, a diet low in saturated fat and cholesterol will help lower the level of blood cholesterol if it is too high. Medications also are available to maintain cholesterol levels within the normal range.

Diabetes: Diabetes appears most frequently during middle age, more often in people who are overweight. In its mild form, diabetes can escape detection for many years, but it can sharply increase a person's risk of heart attack, making control of other risk factors even more important. A doctor can detect diabetes and prescribe changes in eating habits, weight control and exercise programs, and drugs, if necessary, to keep it in check.

Contributing Risk Factors

There are other factors that probably contribute indirectly to heart disease (Figure 8). All three of these risk factors can be eliminated.

Obesity: In most cases, obesity results simply from eating too much and exercising too little. It places a heavy burden on the heart. In addition, obesity is associated with coronary heart disease primarily because of its influence on blood pressure, blood cholesterol, and precipitating diabetes. To reduce weight, doctors usually recommend a program that combines exercise with a low-calorie diet.

Lack of Exercise: Lack of exercise has not been clearly established as a risk factor for heart attack. But when combined with overeating, lack of exercise may lead to excess weight, which is clearly a contributing factor. (A doctor should be consulted prior to commencing any exercise program.)

Excessive Stress: It is virtually impossible to define and measure a person's emotional and mental stress level. All human beings feel stress, but excessive stress over a long period may create health problems in some people. Most doctors agree that reduction of emotional stress will benefit the health of the average individual. A particular way of handling stress has been described as related to increased risk of heart disease,[4] but more data need to be accumulated.

Prudent Heart Living

Prudent heart living is a lifestyle that minimizes the risk of future heart disease. This lifestyle includes weight control, physical fitness, sensible dietary habits, avoidance of cigarette smoking, reduction of blood fats (such as cholesterol and triglycerides), and control of high blood pressure. This section on prudent heart living has been included for those interested in more detailed information about risk factors and their relation to heart disease.

The AHA also publishes a number of other materials concerning prudent heart living; they may be useful as further information for the Instructor and student: *Community Programs Modular Listing of Materials for Health Programming* (AHA 54-005-A); *The American Heart Association Cookbook*, fourth edition; *The American Heart Association Diet* (AHA 51-018-B); and *Cooking Without Your Salt Shaker* (AHA 53-002-A).

A number of large studies are now in progress in this country to establish the effectiveness of risk factor modification in reducing cardiovascular morbidity and mortality. Most authorities believe that risk factor reduction is an important part of any comprehensive approach to reducing cardiovascular illness and death in the community, especially among children and young adults.

While elevated cholesterol, cigarette smoking, and high blood pressure are considered to be the most significant risk factors, others have been identified. They include diabetes, obesity, male gender, heredity, advancing age, and a sedentary lifestyle. A strong family history of premature vascular disease and the presence of diabetes put the individual at higher risk for premature blood vessel disease. Individuals at increased risk because of these factors should make special efforts to minimize their risk by eliminating factors such as smoking and by modifying factors such as high blood pressure.

The living habits of millions of Americans are endangering their hearts at a comparatively early age. Children begin to overeat and develop a taste for foods high in salt and cholesterol and empty in calories. Some are not encouraged to get enough exercise, and television further limits play activity. The smoking habit frequently begins during early teen years, especially if parents smoke. By adulthood many Americans are overweight, lead sedentary lives, and smoke heavily. Many have high levels of cholesterol and triglycerides in their blood. High blood pressure is prevalent.

Most of the scientific evidence available today indicates that reducing risk factors may prevent many heart attacks. At the very least, reducing the risks can result in good general health and physical fitness and can benefit every member of the family. Children benefit most of all by learning the habits of prudent heart living early in life.

Eliminate Cigarette Smoking

Cigarette smoking[5] is a major cause of coronary heart disease in the United States for men. In women who take oral contraceptives containing estrogens, cigarette smoking markedly predisposes to cardiovascular disease. Because of the number of persons in the population who smoke and the increased risk that smoking represents, "cigarette smoking should be considered the most important of the known modifiable risk factors for coronary heart disease in the United States."[5]

Overall, cigarette smokers experience a 70% greater CHD death rate than do nonsmokers. Heavy smokers (two or more packs per day) have CHD death rates between two and three times greater than nonsmokers. The risk of developing CHD increases with increasing exposure to cigarette smoke, as measured by the number of cigarettes smoked daily, the total number of years one has smoked, the degree of inhalation, and how early in life one started smoking. Cigarette smoking is a major independent risk factor, and it acts synergistically with other risk factors (most notably elevated cholesterol and hypertension) to greatly increase the risk of CHD.

Women have lower rates for CHD than do men. In particular, CHD rates for women are lower prior to menopause. A part of this difference is due to the fact that fewer women smoke and those who do tend to smoke fewer cigarettes per day and inhale less deeply. Among women who have smoking patterns comparable to those of men, CHD death rates are similar. Women who use oral contraceptives and who smoke increase their risk of myocardial infarction by approximately tenfold, compared with women who neither use oral contraceptives nor smoke.

Cigarette smoking has been found to elevate the risk of sudden death significantly. Overall, smokers experience a two to four times greater risk of sudden death than nonsmokers. The risk appears to increase with the number of cigarettes smoked per day. It diminishes to almost normal with cessation of smoking.

The CHD mortality ratio of smokers is greater for the younger age groups than for the older age groups. Although the smoker-to-nonsmoker mortality ratio narrows with increasing age, smokers continue to experience greater CHD death rates at all ages.

Cigarette smoking has been estimated to be responsible for up to 30% of all CHD deaths in the United States each year. During the period 1965–1980 there were over three million premature deaths from heart disease in the U.S. attributed to cigarette smoking. Unless smoking habits of the population change, perhaps 10% of all persons now alive may die prematurely of heart disease attributable to their smoking behavior. The total number of such premature deaths may exceed 24 million.

"Warning: The Surgeon General Has Determined That Cigarette Smoking Is Dangerous to Your Health." Many studies have shown that cigarette smokers have a greater risk of dying from a variety of diseases than nonsmokers. If a smoker and a nonsmoker are victims of the same disease, the disease is more likely to be fatal to the smoker. The same studies indicate that people who give up smoking have a lower death rate from heart attack than persistent smokers. After a period of years, the death rate of those who stop smoking is nearly as low as that of people who have never smoked. Some of the abnormal changes in lung tissue of heavy smokers have also been shown to gradually improve.

The earlier a person begins to smoke, the greater the risk to future health. There is considerable pressure on teenagers to smoke, and whether or not they resist may depend on the example set by their parents. It has been shown that in the majority of families where parents do not smoke neither do the children.

Control High Blood Pressure

Almost 58,000,000 adults and children in the United States have high blood pressure or are being treated for high blood pressure by a physician. It affects nearly 1 in every 3 adults.

Certain arteries in the body, called arterioles, regulate blood pressure. They are the smallest branches of the aorta, the main artery leaving the heart, carrying blood in the circulatory system. The manner in which arterioles control blood pressure is sometimes compared to the way a nozzle regulates water pressure in a hose. If the nozzle is turned to make the opening larger, less pressure is needed to force the water through the hose. If the nozzle is turned to make the opening narrower, or smaller, the pressure in the hose increases. Accordingly, thinking of the arterioles as a hose, if they become narrower for any reason, the blood cannot easily pass through. This increases the blood pressure in the arteries and may overwork the heart. If the pressure increases above normal and stays there, the result is high blood pressure, or hypertension.

Primary, or essential, high blood pressure is the most common type. As opposed to secondary hypertension, which is caused by some disease (such as kidney disease), primary hypertension is of unknown origin.

Experts who have studied high blood pressure report that a tendency toward this disease is often found in families. People whose parents had high blood pressure are more likely to develop it than those individuals whose parents did not. If there is a family history of stroke or heart attack at an early age or if parents have high blood pressure, all members of the family should have regular blood pressure checks.

Primary high blood pressure cannot be cured, but it can usually be controlled. Uncontrolled high blood pressure adds to the workload of the heart and arteries. The heart, forced to work harder than normal over a long period, tends to enlarge. A slightly enlarged heart may function well, but a heart that is very much enlarged has a hard time keeping up with the demands made on it.

As people grow older, the arteries and their smaller branches, the arterioles, become hardened and less elastic (arteriosclerosis). This process takes place gradually, even in people who do not have high blood pressure. However, high blood pressure tends to speed up this hardening process.

The possibility of stroke — blood vessel damage in the brain — is increased with high blood pressure. Uncontrolled high blood pressure can also affect the kidneys.

All of these effects on the heart, kidneys, and brain are called end-organ damage and can be prevented or reduced if high blood pressure is treated early — and if this treatment is continued.

Moderate elevations of blood pressure may be controlled by sodium and weight reduction. The optimal degree of sodium reduction has not yet been completely established. Table salt is 40% sodium. By removing the salt shaker from the table and not adding salt while cooking, salt consumption can be significantly reduced. A physician's advice should be obtained about weight reduction. For persons with severe hypertension or with mild-to-moderate hypertension not controlled by these measures, antihypertensive drugs can be used. Blood pressure needs to be controlled long-term.

Decrease Blood Cholesterol Levels

Cholesterol is the main lipid-like (fat) component of the atherosclerotic deposits. An elevation of the total blood cholesterol level (hypercholesterolemia) has been consistently associated with coronary heart disease. Although hypercholesterolemia is sometimes a family trait, it is often due to environmental factors, the most influential being diet. Studies in humans have shown that the serum cholesterol level can be raised in most individuals by ingestion of saturated fat and cholesterol and lowered by substantially reducing this intake.

The National Heart, Lung, and Blood Institute[6, 7] investigated the effect of cholesterol lowering on risk of CHD in 3,806 men for 7 years in the Coronary Primary Prevention Trial. Two groups were studied, both receiving a diet that lowered cholesterol by 4.0%. One group received the drug cholestyramine that lowered cholesterol by an additional 8.5%. The group with the lower cholesterol level had a 24% reduction in CHD and a 19% reduction in heart attacks. This is the first conclusive evidence that a reduction in cholesterol by drug treatment can decrease the incidence of CHD and heart attack.

An elevation of serum triglyceride (the main fatty substance in the fluid portion of blood) may also be associated with an increased risk of CHD, although this relation is not as well established as in the case of cholesterol.

Cholesterol is a substance that is manufactured by the body but also present in the foods we eat. It is found in especially large amounts in egg yolk and organ meats. Shrimp and lobster are moderately high in cholesterol. Excess cholesterol is deposited in the arteries and may lead to atherosclerosis.

Saturated fats raise cholesterol blood levels in most individuals. The major sources of saturated fats are meat, animal fats, some vegetable oils (palm kernel oil, coconut oil, cocoa butter, and heavily hydrogenated margarines and shortenings), dairy products (whole milk, cream, butter, ice cream, and cheese), and bakery goods. Polyunsaturated fats, on the other hand, tend to lower the level of cholesterol. The goal is to keep the total amount of fat, as well as just saturated fat, low in the diet. By partially substituting polyunsaturated fats for saturated fat and by increasing the amount of complex carbohydrates in the diet, it is possible to achieve the goal. The following points are illustrations of what these recommendations mean in terms of food:

- Eat fish or poultry more frequently than red meat, using no more than 6 ounces per day. When you do prepare red meat (beef, pork, lamb), use lean cuts, trim off excess fat, and serve small portions. Do not eat the "skin" of poultry.
- Cook with liquid vegetable oils and polyunsaturated, nonhydrogenated margarines (e.g., corn, cottonseed, soybean, and safflower products).
- Use skimmed milk products.
- Eat fewer eggs, preferably no more than three egg yolks per week.
- Use low-fat cooking methods such as baking, broiling, and roasting.

Changes in diet should never be drastic. Elimination of essential foods can be harmful. Fad diets that totally exclude one type of food from the diet can lead to additional health problems. However, with moderate changes in diet and careful monitoring of cholesterol and saturated fats, blood cholesterol can usually be kept at acceptable levels.

It is generally accepted that atherosclerosis may begin in childhood, progress through young adulthood, and become manifest only in middle age or later. It is therefore recommended that children over 2 years old follow the same dietary guidelines that are recommended herein for adults.[8]

Control Diabetes

Diabetes, or a familial tendency toward diabetes, is associated with an increased risk of CHD. The risk of CHD is twice as great in diabetic men and three times as great in diabetic women as in persons free of this disease. Diabetic women may have as great a mortality from coronary heart disease as nondiabetic men of the same age. The control of hyperglycemia (increased blood sugar) alone does not appear to reduce the risk of the large blood vessel involvement of diabetes.[9] The diabetic should direct close attention to the management of commonly associated risk factors (hypercholesterolemia, hypertriglyceridemia, hypertension, and obesity).

Eliminate Obesity

Obesity is associated with an increased occurrence of CHD, particularly angina pectoris and sudden death, largely as a consequence of its influence on blood pressure, blood lipids, and the risk of diabetes. There is some evidence to indicate that obesity may directly contribute to coronary heart disease. Few persons become obese without developing a less favorable coronary risk profile.

Most people reach their normal adult weight between the ages of 21 and 25. With each succeeding year, fewer calories are needed to maintain this weight. People in their 30's and 40's who eat as much as they did in their early 20's and who become physically less active will store the excess calories as body fat.

It has been shown that life expectancy may be shorter for people who are markedly overweight. Middle-aged men who are significantly overweight have about three times the risk of a fatal heart attack as middle-aged men of normal weight. Obesity also means greater risk of hypertension and diabetes.

There is no quick, easy way to lose weight. Extreme reducing diets are best avoided because they usually exclude foods essential to good health. Even when these diets do lower weight, patterns of eating that will help maintain normal weight are not developed. The physician will know the best weight for a given height, age, and build and is the best source of advice for weight reduction.

Get More Exercise

Some studies have shown that men who lead sedentary lives run a higher risk of heart attack than those who exercise regularly. Studies have also suggested that a prudent exercise program may be beneficial as part of a comprehensive risk reduction program. Regular exercise can increase cardiovascular functional capacity and may decrease myocardial oxygen demand for any given level of physical activity. The risk of vigorous physical activity may be reduced by appropriate medical evaluation.

Exercise tones the muscles, stimulates the circulation, helps prevent obesity, and promotes a general feeling of well-being. There is some evidence to suggest that the survival rate of heart attack victims is higher in those who have exercised regularly than those who have not.

People of all ages should develop a physically active lifestyle as part of a comprehensive program of heart disease prevention. Especially valuable are aerobic activities requiring movement of body weight over distance — walking, stair-climbing, running, cycling, swimming, or similar activities. For those who exercise infrequently, isometric activities such as weightlifting should be avoided because of their strenuous nature. Improvements in cardiovascular fitness appear to result from regular exercise of moderate intensity (50–75% of capacity) when performed 15–30 minutes at least every other day. Vigorous exercise should be prescribed with caution for high-risk persons. Graded exercise tolerance tests, which may be used to help in formulating an individual's exercise prescription, should be performed under medical supervision.

Strenuous and unaccustomed activity, however, occasionally brings on a heart attack in an apparently healthy person who has undiagnosed heart disease. Before undertaking an exercise program or engaging in heavy physical labor, a physician should be consulted. An exercise test may be part of the evaluation of the individual's physical condition. Physical activity should be increased gradually in any exercise program. If the physician indicates the person is physically fit, introducing an enjoyable sport into the lifestyle can be beneficial.

Reduce Stress

The stresses of modern society are often mentioned as a risk factor. Social and professional stress may provoke other risk factors (for example, cause a rise in blood pressure or blood cholesterol), lead to excessive smoking or eating, or perhaps induce coronary thrombosis. However, stress levels are difficult to measure, and responses to stress vary markedly. It has been suggested that persons with an overdeveloped sense of time urgency, drive, or competitiveness are more prone to heart attack than those who are more complacent and do not respond excessively to stresses. This is an issue that requires further investigation.

Clinical Syndromes of Coronary Heart Disease

Individuals with coronary artery disease may be asymptomatic (no signs or signals) or symptomatic. In an individual with asymptomatic coronary artery disease (Figure 9), the process of coronary artery narrowing progresses over time. This is the period before enough decrease in blood supply occurs to produce symptoms of heart disease. Symptomatic coronary artery disease can be divided into three categories: angina pectoris, myocardial infarction (heart attack), and sudden cardiac death.

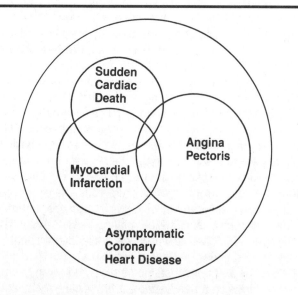

Figure 9. Clinical syndromes of coronary heart disease.

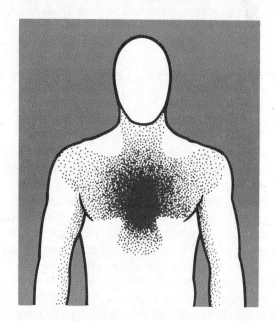

Figure 10. Intensity and location of pain as a symptom of coronary heart disease.

Angina Pectoris

Angina pectoris is a transient pain or discomfort due to a temporary imbalance between the demand for oxygen by the heart muscle and the ability of the coronary arteries to supply enough blood to meet that demand. It may be central (retrosternal) or more diffuse — i.e., throughout the anterior chest — and is usually described as being crushing, pressing, constricting, oppressive, or heavy (Figure 10). It may radiate to one (more often the left) or both shoulders and/or arms or to the neck, jaw, back, or epigastrium (upper midportion of abdomen). Discomfort occurring in the arms, shoulders, neck, jaw, back, or epigastrium without anterior chest discomfort may also be a manifestation of angina. It is a steady discomfort, most commonly lasting 2–10 or 15 minutes, precipitated by any factor that increases oxygen demand or decreases oxygen supply of the heart. The most frequent cause of angina is coronary atherosclerosis. Commonly, angina is initially precipitated by exertion, which increases both heart rate and blood pressure. As the magnitude of coronary artery narrowing increases, the amount of exertion needed to precipitate angina decreases. It is promptly relieved by rest and/or nitroglycerin. With severe coronary artery disease, angina may occur at rest.

Acute Myocardial Infarction (Heart Attack)

Heart attack occurs when the demand of the heart muscle (myocardium) for blood (oxygen) far exceeds the supply. It usually results from severe narrowing or complete blockage of a diseased coronary artery and results in death of the heart muscle cells supplied by that artery. Spasm of one or more of the diseased vessels also has been implicated as a causative factor. The injury to the muscle results in electrical instability that may lead to altered electrical rhythms, including ventricular fibrillation. The usual symptom (signal) of a heart attack is a pressure or pain in the chest that persists for two minutes or longer and is not relieved promptly by rest and/or nitroglycerin.

Definition

Acute myocardial infarction means "death of the heart muscle" due to inadequate oxygen and is another term for heart attack. Inadequate blood (oxygen) supply can be due to a clot in the coronary artery or narrowing due to atherosclerotic plaque. "Coronary" and "coronary thrombosis" are old-fashioned terms for heart attack caused by a blood clot in a coronary artery.

Precipitating Events

In a study that examined patient activity at the onset of myocardial infarction, 59% were either at rest or asleep while 31% were involved in mild-to-moderate, or usual, exercise.[10] Comparable data fail to support a cause-and-effect relation between vigorous exertion and myocardial infarction[11] although contradictory evidence has been offered.[11-16] The combination of severe exertion and excessive fatigue or unusual emotional stress has been incriminated as more likely to precipitate myocardial infarction.[12] Emotional stress and life events with a powerful impact on the individual, e.g., death of a significant other person, divorce, or loss of job, continue to be observed commonly prior to myocardial infarction and may be correlated.[17, 18]

Warning Signs

Chest discomfort or pain is the most significant signal of a heart attack. Important parameters of the pain of heart attack are as follows:

1. Character: Uncomfortable pressure, squeezing, fullness, tightness, aching, crushing, constriction, oppression, or heaviness.
2. Location: In the center of the chest behind the breastbone. It may spread to one or both shoulders, arms, neck, jaw, or back.
3. Duration: The discomfort of a heart attack will usually last longer than 2 minutes. It may come and go.

Other signs may include any or all of the following: sweating, nausea, or shortness of breath. A feeling of weakness may accompany the chest discomfort. However, be alert to the fact that 1) the pain may not be severe, 2) the person does not necessarily have to "look bad" or have all the symptoms before action is taken, and 3) sharp, stabbing twinges of pain are usually not signals of a heart attack.

The signals can occur in either sex, even in young adults, at any time and in any place. Physical or emotional stress are not necessarily precipitating factors of a heart attack.

Actions for Survival

Many heart attack deaths occur before victims reach the hospital. A great number of these fatalities could be prevented if the victim responded quickly, preferably within the first 2 minutes after the onset of the signs and signals. The usual cause of death in a heart attack is electrical instability of the heart. This instability, which can lead to an arrhythmia (abnormal heart rhythm), is common and begins with the onset of myocardial injury. (*Heart Attack Signals and Actions for Survival*, AHA 70-039-A, can be presented as a separate program.)

Prevention is the best medicine, but in spite of efforts to educate the public about risk factors and early warning signals of heart attack, the rate of death from this major killer continues at an appalling level. More than half of all heart attack victims die outside the hospital, most within 2 hours of initial symptoms. It is essential to know and to be able to recognize the signals of heart attack.

The initial treatment should be to have the patient rest quietly and calmly. Since both angina pectoris and heart attack are caused by an inability of the coronary circulation to meet the oxygen demand (too little oxygen to the

heart muscle), activity must be kept at a minimum. When heart rate or blood pressure increases, such as during activity, the heart requires more oxygen. Rest keeps these at a minimum. The patient should be allowed to assume the position, either lying down or sitting up, that allows the most comfort and easiest breathing.

The victim's first tendency is to deny the possibility of a heart attack with such rationalizations as the following: It's indigestion or something I ate; it can't happen to me; I'm too healthy; I don't want to bother my doctor; I'm under no strain; I don't want to frighten anyone; I'll take a home remedy; I'll feel ridiculous if it isn't a heart attack. When the victim starts looking for reasons why he can't be having a heart attack, it is a signal for positive action.

If the typical chest discomfort lasts for 2 minutes or more, emergency action should be initiated. The exception would be with a known heart patient with instructions from his physician to take nitroglycerin first. Nitroglycerin tablets or spray under the tongue or nitroglycerin ointment on the skin may relieve the pain of angina pectoris. Nitroglycerin acts by both 1) dilating the coronary arteries, which increases blood flow to the heart muscle, and 2) lowering the blood pressure and dilating the veins, which decreases the work of the heart and the heart muscle's need for oxygen.

Since nitroglycerin lowers the blood pressure, it should be given with the victim sitting or lying. It usually produces a stinging sensation under the tongue and may cause a headache. (Note: Nitroglycerin tablets may be inactivated by age and light. It is best to keep a fresh supply in a dark place and carry only a few tablets in a small, dark bottle, changing to fresh tablets every month or so.)

Even in known heart patients, if typical symptoms persist for 10 minutes despite rest and three nitroglycerin tablets, an emergency *action plan* should be followed (Figure 11).

For a person with unknown coronary heart disease:

1. Recognize the signals.
2. Stop activity and sit or lie down.
3. If pain persists for two minutes or more, call the EMS system. (Dial 911 or the local emergency number.) If the EMS system is not available, the patient should be taken immediately to the nearest hospital emergency room that provides 24-hour emergency cardiac care.

For a person with known coronary heart disease using nitroglycerin:

1. Recognize the signals.
2. Stop activity and sit or lie down.
3. Place one nitroglycerin tablet or spray sublingually — repeat at 3- to 5-minute intervals to a total dose of three tablets if discomfort is not relieved. (Lay rescuers should be very cautious when administering a victim's nitroglycerin because the victim may already have taken some nitroglycerin and because tablet strengths may vary with the individual.)

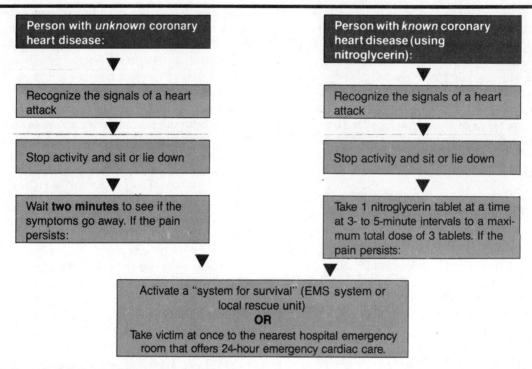

Figure 11. Emergency action plan for person with signals of heart attack.

4. If signals persist, call the EMS system. If an EMS system is not available, the victim should be taken to the nearest hospital emergency room that provides 24-hour emergency cardiac care.

Individuals should have an emergency *action plan* at home and at work:

1. Know the appropriate emergency rescue service telephone number (usually 911).
2. Know the location of the nearest hospital emergency room that provides 24-hour emergency cardiac care.
3. Discuss with the family physician the hospital of choice, distance to be traveled, and emergency facilities of hospitals under consideration.

Because the victim may deny the possibility of a heart attack, it is essential that the person nearest at the time activate emergency action and be prepared to render basic life support if necessary.

The person who is with the individual having signals that last for 2 minutes or longer should act quickly. Expect a denial — but insist on taking prompt action:

1. Call the EMS system. If not available:
2. Take the victim to the nearest hospital emergency room that provides 24-hour emergency cardiac care.
3. Be prepared to provide CPR (rescue breathing and chest compression) if necessary. Training is the only way to be prepared.

Monitor the patient continuously by feeling the pulse. Electrocardiographic monitoring should be initiated as soon as possible. Oxygen should be administered, if available, by ACLS personnel. Without warning, the patient may develop a rhythm disturbance that causes cardiac arrest.

Sudden Cardiac Death (Cardiac Arrest)

"Sudden death" occurs when heartbeat and breathing stop abruptly or unexpectedly. Sudden cardiac death, or cardiac arrest, may occur as the initial and only manifestation of coronary artery disease. Sudden cardiac death may occur before any other symptom of a heart attack. It may also occur in individuals with known coronary artery disease, and especially during a heart attack. It most commonly occurs within 1 or 2 hours after the beginning of a heart attack.

There are numerous noncardiac causes of sudden death that are discussed later.

Within seconds after cardiac arrest occurs, the victim loses consciousness and breathing stops. During this early phase, the victim may have a convulsion. The sooner circulation to the brain is restored, the greater the chance for full recovery of brain function. After 4–6 minutes of cardiac arrest, significant brain damage usually occurs. Children, especially infants, and victims of drowning and cold exposure may recover normal brain function after longer periods of cardiac arrest. (The infant's brain is more resistant to injury from lack of oxygen; victims of drowning and cold exposure may be protected by the lower body temperature.) Any individual who has sustained cardiac arrest may be kept alive with basic life support.

Causes

Coronary heart disease is the most common cause of cardiac arrest. Yet, any condition that interferes with the delivery of oxygen (respiratory arrest) or blood to the coronary circulation (shock) or that causes depression or irritation of the heart muscle itself (direct injury to the heart, drugs, cardiac rhythm disturbance) may lead to cardiac arrest. Since the heart does not require normal brain function to continue beating, brain injury by itself does not necessarily lead to cardiac arrest. It is generally the respiratory arrest resulting from brain injury that causes cardiac arrest. Once respiration ceases, however, the heart may continue to beat for several minutes until the oxygen level in the blood is so low that cardiac depression occurs. Then cardiac arrest may follow.

Most often the direct cause of the cardiac arrest is ventricular fibrillation (a chaotic, uncoordinated quivering of the heart muscle). Although it is accompanied by evidence of electrical activity, there is no effective heartbeat. This chaotic activity is caused by electrical interference from the area of injured heart muscle, and normal coordinated electrical and mechanical activity is interrupted.

Individuals who have been successfully resuscitated from sudden death have usually been found to have significant coronary artery disease, but many do not show evidence of heart attack (death of heart muscle). It is probable that the marked oxygen supply–demand imbalance causes electrical instability of the heart muscle, causing ventricular fibrillation.

In cardiac arrest due to ventricular fibrillation, the abnormal rhythm seldom can be converted to an effective heart beat without electrical defibrillation, although CPR may keep the victim's brain alive in the interim.

Defibrillation is the application of electric shock to a fibrillating heart that momentarily stops all electrical activity and allows spontaneous coordinated electrical and mechanical function to return, thus producing an effective heartbeat. Defibrillation should be performed by appropriately trained personnel at the scene.

If CPR is initiated promptly and the patient is successfully defibrillated, there is a good chance for survival.

The Role of Prevention

As important as it is to provide emergency treatment for the cardiac arrest victim, it is equally important to remain aware that, however effective and idealized emergency cardiac care for the prehospital cardiac arrest victim can become, prevention of cardiac arrest is a far more desirable approach. A shift in the burden of responsibility to the layperson very likely will prove an essential element in effective coronary heart disease mortality reduction. Control of recognized risk factors depends very much on the willingness of the public to accept the responsibility and consequences of its behavior. Part of this acceptance may depend on the amount and type of exposure to risk factor information and the extent to which the layperson can be brought to appreciate the personal relevance of risk factor change. Evidence now exists that community-wide campaigns can be effective in reducing cardiovascular risks.

In addition, educational efforts should be directed toward overcoming patients' intrinsic denial of early evidence of cardiac disease as well as encouraging rapid entrance into the EMS system when symptoms of coronary heart disease develop.

The Role of Resuscitation

Clearly, cardiopulmonary resuscitation can be an effective approach to cardiac arrest. A critical link in the successful implementation of out-of-hospital resuscitation is the trained layperson. Several studies have documented the increasing incidence of successful resuscitation of the out-of-hospital cardiac arrest victim (in many cases by trained bystanders) when CPR is begun within 1 or 2 minutes after the development of ventricular fibrillation.[19-22]

It is clear from these and other observations that BLS, consisting of rescue breathing and external chest compressions, must be complemented by rapid delivery of ACLS (Table 1). This includes the capability of defibrillation as well as nearly all other aspects of definitive ECC if an important impact is to be made on out-of-hospital cardiac arrest mortality. Successful resuscitation has been observed in up to 61% of selected subgroups of out-of-hospital cardiac arrest victims when layperson CPR and an effective emergency response system capable of providing ACLS have been available within the community.[19] Thus, there are two indispensable ingredients in the aggressive approach to out-of-hospital cardiac arrest: 1) layperson education and training in CPR and 2) a mobile emergency cardiac care capability that can be available within minutes to the victim of cardiac arrest.

Table 1. Relation of Survival Rates from Cardiac Arrest (Ventricular Fibrillation) to Promptness of CPR and ACLS.[23] (Used by permission.)

Initiation of CPR (Minutes)	Arrival of ACLS (Minutes)	Survival Rate (%)
0–4	0–8	43
0–4	16+	10
8–12	8–16	6
8–12	16+	0
12+	12+	0

Events Requiring Resuscitation: An Overview

There are many clinical syndromes that necessitate resuscitative efforts (Figure 12). CPR is indicated in any situation where either breathing or both breathing and heartbeat are absent.

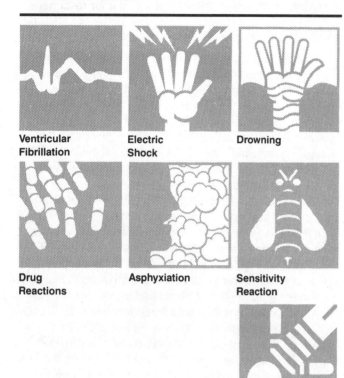

Ventricular Fibrillation

Electric Shock

Drowning

Drug Reactions

Asphyxiation

Sensitivity Reaction

Trauma

Figure 12. Some common causes of sudden death.

Causes of Absent Breathing

Several factors can precipitate absence of breath:

1. Obstruction of the airway. Breathing eventually will stop from lack of oxygen. The tongue and epiglottis are the most common causes of an airway obstruction. Foreign body obstruction of the airway is also common, especially in children: Food, toys, coins, and the like may become lodged in the airway, making it impossible to inhale or exhale air. If the airway is totally blocked, hypoxia (lack of oxygen) will ensue and cause all breathing efforts to stop. Cardiac arrest will subsequently occur.
2. Brain injury. Trauma, stroke, drug overdose, and severe shock can depress the respiratory center and in this way suppress the respiratory drive.
3. Chest wall injury with paralysis or severe lung injury.

4. Various drugs. Antipsychotics and antidepressants can act on the respiratory center and suppress the stimulus to breathe.
5. Electrocution.
6. Drowning.
7. Cardiac arrest. Within seconds after a patient has a cardiac arrest, the respiratory center will be without oxygen and breathing will stop.

In cases of respiratory arrest alone, rescue breathing may be enough to restore spontaneous breathing and/or prevent cardiac arrest.

Causes of Absent Circulation

Factors that can cause or contribute to the absence of circulation include the following:

1. Cardiac arrest. This condition can be recognized by absence of pulse and can result from a) ventricular fibrillation, b) ventricular standstill (asystole), the absence of both electrical activity and cardiac muscle contraction, and c) electromechanical dissociation, the presence of electrical activity but ineffective muscle contraction. These electrical mechanisms, all of which result in an absence of pulse, can be differentiated only by electrocardiography, but the initial treatment is CPR.
2. Severe shock due to massive loss of blood.
3. Trauma to the heart.
4. Drugs that cause arrhythmias or depression of the contractions of the heart muscle.
5. Respiratory arrest. If respiration ceases, it will eventually lead to cardiac arrest. The heart may continue to beat for a few minutes until the level of oxygen in the blood to the coronary arteries becomes so low that normal cardiac function cannot continue. Cardiac arrest will follow.

Two Definitions of Death

Two definitions of death aid in the understanding of the role of CPR and the possibility for survival:

Clinical death means that the heartbeat and breathing have stopped. This process is *reversible*. ("Sudden death" is abrupt or unexpected clinical death.)

Biological death is permanent cellular damage due to lack of oxygen. (The brain cells are the most sensitive to the lack of oxygen.) This process is *final*.

A person may be pronounced legally dead during either clinical or biological death. But during that first few minutes, promptly initiated CPR (BLS and ACLS) may turn the clinical death victim back to productive life. Without CPR, biological death will occur.

In every case of arrested breathing or cardiac arrest, time is critical. There is usually enough oxygen in the lungs and bloodstream to support life for up to 6 minutes. When breathing stops first, the heart will continue to pump blood for several minutes. Existing oxygen in the victim's lungs will continue to be circulated through the

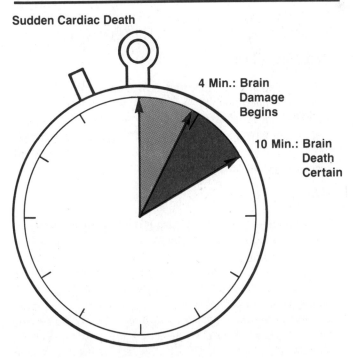

Sudden Cardiac Death

4 Min.: Brain Damage Begins

10 Min.: Brain Death Certain

Figure 13. Time is critical in starting CPR.

bloodstream to the brain and other vital organs. When the heart stops, however, the oxygen in the lungs and blood-stream cannot be circulated to the vital organs.

The victim whose heart and breathing have been interrupted for less than 4 minutes has an excellent chance for full recovery if CPR is administered immediately and followed by ACLS within the next 4 minutes (Figure 13). In the period from 4 to 6 minutes brain damage may occur. After 6 minutes brain damage will almost always occur.

For these reasons it is critically important for the nearest person to

1. Recognize the need for immediate action
2. Perform the proper steps of CPR effectively

Special Situations for CPR: Noncardiac Causes of Sudden Death

The cause of sudden death is not always cardiac in origin. Some of the more common other causes are discussed below in some detail.

Near Drowning

Approximately 6,000 persons drown in the United States each year.[2] Common patterns of drowning include children falling into backyard swimming pools; underwater blackout by experienced swimmers who have hyperventilated before attempting an underwater long-distance goal; and fatal accidents involving persons who drink alcohol, then go swimming and boating.[24] It is important to emphasize that a near-drowning victim may recover completely after extended periods of submersion. The com-

monly considered 4- to 6-minute limit for brain survival is not applicable in the drowning victim because of the protective effects of low-temperature water and the "diving" reflex. Successful resuscitation with full neurological recovery has occurred in near-drowning victims with prolonged submersion in cold water.[25, 26] An absolute time limit beyond which resuscitation is not indicated has not been established. Since it is often difficult for rescuers to obtain an accurate time of submersion, attempts at resuscitation should be initiated by rescuers at the scene unless there is obvious physical evidence of death (such as putrefaction).

Hypothermia (decrease in core body temperature) may be protective due to a slowing metabolic rate causing decreased oxygen use. Further, the diving reflex is a physiological response that man shares with certain birds and mammals equipped to stay under water for long periods of time.[27] When a person's face is immersed in cold water, a reflex is immediately activated that slows the heart rate and constricts peripheral arteries, shunting blood away from the gut and extremities and sending it to the brain and heart. The combination of the diving reflex and the cold, which reduces oxygen requirements, contributes to the protection of submersion victims and may substantially increase the time until irreversible brain damage develops. Because of this protective mechanism, resuscitative efforts should be attempted for submersion victims even if more than 4–6 minutes are known to have elapsed.

The drowning victim initially panics, and this is followed by an exhausting struggle to stay above the surface and to reach safety. Frantic hyperventilation, breathholding during submersion, water-swallowing, vomiting, violent coughing, and finally, involuntary gasps resulting in the flooding of the air passages and lungs may lead to unconsciousness, convulsions, and death.

Because of spasm of the vocal cords (laryngospasm), about 10% of drowning victims do not aspirate water into their lungs.

Hypothermia

Hypothermia may occur because of 1) environmental exposure (cold-water drowning; exposure to low temperatures without protection, especially in alcoholics and hikers) or 2) a total failure of the body's temperature-regulating system (alcohol, sedatives, antidepressants, neurologic problems in the elderly). A hypothermic state is present if the core body temperature falls to less than 90° F (32° C). Multiple changes take place in the body in a hypothermic state, the most important of which is a decrease in metabolic rate, which in turn causes a decrease in the amount of oxygen used by the body. The heart rate slows and the amount of blood pumped decreases. Brain activity decreases as the temperature is lowered, thus decreasing brain oxygen requirements. For this reason, the severely hypothermic patient can withstand longer periods of cardiopulmonary arrest than the patient with normal temperature. The status of the victim's circulatory and respiratory system may be hard to assess because of slow pulse, slow breathing, and dilated pupils. During initial assessment a longer time to check for a pulse (up to 1 minute) may be necessary.[28] CPR should be instituted in any case in which the rescuer cannot detect breathing and pulse. Prolonged resuscitation efforts should continue until near normal temperature has returned. Subsequent, supportive measures should be instituted as indicated.[29] The victim should be transported, with continued CPR, as quickly as possible to an advanced life support treatment facility.

Allergies

Fortunately, severe allergic reactions are rare, but when they occur the consequences may be life-threatening. Exposure to a known allergen (foods, pollens, etc.) or a reaction to an insect bite (e.g., bee stings) may be the initial inciting event. Upper airway obstruction due to laryngeal edema and anaphylactic shock (life-threatening cardiovascular collapse) are the most severe consequences of an allergic reaction. The rescuer should initiate CPR as with any other cause of arrest.

Electric Shock

Persons working with or near high-voltage power lines or electricity at home or work may be subject to accidental electrocution. Complications that may follow an electric shock depend largely on the amplitude and duration of contact with the current. Electrical burns and injuries caused by falling may require prompt attention; and some consequences are likely to require CPR:

1. Tetany of the breathing muscles. This is usually limited to the duration of current exposure. If current exposure is prolonged and tetany persists, cardiac arrest may occur because of hypoxia.
2. Prolonged paralysis of the breathing muscles. This may result from massive convulsive phenomena that last for minutes after the shock current has terminated and result in hypoxic cardiac arrest.
3. Cardiac arrest. Ventricular fibrillation or ventricular asystole may occur as a direct result of electric shock, and both require CPR. Other serious cardiac arrhythmias, including ventricular tachycardia that may progress to ventricular fibrillation, may result from exposure to low- or high-voltage currents sustained for several seconds and may require ACLS monitoring and treatment or resuscitation.

The prognosis for victims of electric shock is not readily predictable, since the amplitude and duration of the charge are not usually known. Failure of either respiration or circulation is likely to result — but not always immediately.

The rescuer must be prepared to institute appropriate CPR but must take care not to become an additional victim by inadvertent contact with the same electrical source. If the victim is still in contact with electrical energy, the rescuer must de-energize the circuit prior to attempting resuscitation.

A recent report[30] on the electric-shock victim located at the top of a utility pole indicates that CPR should be instituted after the victim is lowered to the ground.

Asphyxiation

Asphyxiation (suffocation) is most commonly caused by inhaling a gas other than air or oxygen. It may occur during fires or from chemical spills or gas leaks. The result is insufficient oxygen to the body, resulting in unconsciousness and, ultimately, cardiopulmonary arrest. Appropriate CPR should be performed.

Trauma

Injuries resulting from any trauma — car accidents, falls, or wounds — may result in cardiac or respiratory arrest. The victim must be handled with extreme care (see Chapter 4) to prevent further injury. Evaluation of the situation and initiation, if necessary, of appropriate CPR techniques may be lifesaving.

Survival from cardiac arrest due to traumatic injury is generally poor.[31-36] External chest compressions may not provide adequate circulation in the severely hypovolemic trauma arrest victim.[32] Emphasis should be placed on rapid transport of such patients to a trauma center where circulating blood volume can be restored and the underlying vascular injury corrected.

Stroke

Information on stroke and, in the next section, epilepsy is provided since they may present signs similar to those of a person in cardiac arrest and may require CPR. Neither topic is required for presentation to students, but special interest groups may have need for the information.

Anatomy of the Cerebral Circulation (Cerebrovascular System)

Oxygen and nutrients (mainly glucose) are supplied to the brain by two major arterial systems. They are the right and left carotid arteries, which run up the front of the neck on either side of the windpipe, and the right and left vertebral arteries, which run up the back of the neck (Figure 14). The branches of these blood vessels unite on the lower surface of the brain to form a circle (Circle of Willis) from which other arteries (anterior cerebral, middle cerebral, posterior cerebral) branch off to supply blood to the brain. Although the brain accounts for only about 2% of total body weight, it receives about 20% of the total blood pumped by the heart. This is to support the high metabolic rate of the brain cells.

Blood is returned from the brain primarily by way of two large veins (right and left internal jugular veins) that run alongside the carotid arteries in the neck.

The brain blood flow is higher in children than it is in adults. During adulthood blood flow decreases with age.

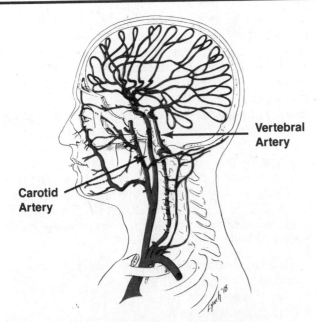

Figure 14. The two major arteries that provide blood to the brain. (Adapted from Morris' *Human Anatomy*, p. 643. Used by permission.)

Risk Factors and Prevention of Stroke

The magnitude of the problem of stroke is great.[3, 37-42] Each year approximately 500,000 people in the United States have a stroke and 155,400 of those persons die, making it the third leading cause of death in the United States. It is estimated that there are a total of 1,960,000 survivors of stroke, many of whom require continuing care and/or rehabilitation.[3]

The major risk factors for stroke include some that cannot be altered, i.e., advanced age, male gender. Others can be treated:

1. High blood pressure (hypertension)
2. Heart disease[37, 38]
   a. Coronary heart disease
   b. Atrial fibrillation (an abnormal heartbeat of the atrium)
   c. Disease of the heart valves
3. Transient ischemic attacks (see "Disease of the Cerebral Vessels")
4. Diabetes

Since most of the major risk factors associated with stroke are potentially treatable, the most important step in preventing stroke is for the individual to recognize the presence of a risk factor and seek proper treatment.

High blood pressure is the major risk factor for stroke. A person whose blood pressure is very high is four times as likely to have a stroke as is a person with normal blood pressure, and even moderately increased pressure is associated with a risk twice that of normal (Figure 15). Every person should have frequent blood pressure checks, and for even moderately elevated blood pressure, medical attention for further evaluation and possible treatment should be sought.

Another important risk factor is *heart disease*. The chance of having a heart attack may be reduced by knowing the risk factors associated with heart disease and following the suggestions for prudent heart living. People with abnormal heart valves and/or an abnormal heart beat (atrial fibrillation) are, in addition, at increased risk for stroke; rheumatic heart disease affects the heart valves.

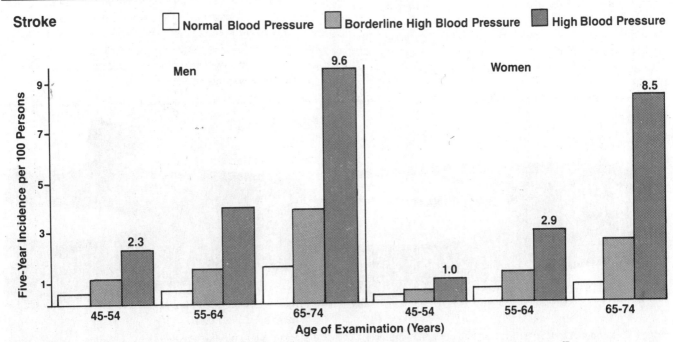

Figure 15. Number of strokes per 100 persons aged 45 to 74 in a recent 5-year period. (Adapted from Kannel WB et al.[37] Used by permission.)

Approximately 25–40% of people who have *transient ischemic attacks* ("little strokes") will go on to have a major stroke within 5 years.[41] Therefore, anyone who has any of the symptoms listed under "Transient Ischemic Attacks" should follow the action plan for the person with the warning signals of stroke.

Diabetes is an important risk factor both for stroke and for heart attack. It often appears in middle age, more frequently in people who are overweight. A doctor can detect diabetes and can prescribe weight control, changes in eating habits, and if necessary, drugs for its treatment.

Disease of the Cerebral Vessels

Disease of the cerebral vessels is caused most commonly by atherosclerosis (see previous section on "Coronary Artery Disease.") A stroke may occur if the buildup of fatty deposits in a cerebral artery becomes so great that it produces a complete or nearly complete blockage of the artery, obstructing blood flow and depriving the brain of oxygen (Figure 16). If a clot forms in a narrowed cerebral vessel, it is called a cerebral thrombosis, and the material that blocks the artery is a thrombus. Strokes may also occur if a piece of the fatty deposit breaks off and travels in the bloodstream until it lodges in one of the smaller arteries supplying the brain. The broken-off piece is called an embolus. Both thrombi and emboli may be said to produce cerebrovascular occlusion leading to cerebral ischemia (lack of blood to the brain).

A stroke may also be caused by hemorrhage. In this case the blood vessel wall ruptures and blood leaks out into or around the brain (Figure 17). This may occur in older persons with atherosclerosis and hypertension but is a less frequent cause of stroke in these individuals than is cerebral thrombosis or embolus. Hemorrhage may also occur secondary to a head injury or the rupture of a cerebral aneurysm. An aneurysm is due to a weak spot in the wall of a cerebral artery. A balloon-like sac filled with blood develops at the site of the weakness. The wall of the sac is very thin and may rupture. Although the weak-

ness in the blood vessel wall is present at birth, the aneurysm often does not develop until later in childhood or adulthood. Nevertheless, both head injuries and cerebral aneurysms may cause strokes in young people.

Transient Ischemic Attacks: A transient ischemic attack (TIA) is an episode in which the symptoms of a stroke occur but last for only a few minutes to a few hours. The individual recovers completely. However, about 25–40% of people who have one or more TIAs later develop a major stroke.[41] Thus, transient ischemic attacks are important early warning signs of stroke. Unfortunately, a large percent of stroke victims do not have prior TIAs.

Signs and Signals: Signs and signals of transient ischemic attacks include the sudden onset of one or more of the following symptoms without other explanation and lasting for at least 30 seconds:

- Weakness, clumsiness, or numbness of the arm, leg, or face
- Loss of speech
- Loss of vision in one eye

Actions for Survival: An individual who experiences a transient ischemic attack should seek medical attention, as the episode may be the forerunner of further TIAs or of a major stroke. While the symptoms will usually have disappeared by the time the person is seen by a physician, tests can be performed that will identify the nature and extent of the cerebral vessel disease and allow the physician to plan medical or surgical therapy to prevent further TIAs and/or a stroke.

Stroke: *Signs and Signals:* The signals of a major stroke are the same as those of a transient ischemic attack except that they do not disappear within a few minutes to a few hours but, instead, remain stable or worsen. In addition, two other signals must be added to the list since the rupture of an aneurysm often produces only 1) a severe headache ("the worst headache of my life") followed, in many instances, by 2) loss of consciousness — with none of the other symptoms listed under "Transient Ischemic Attacks."

Blood Clot

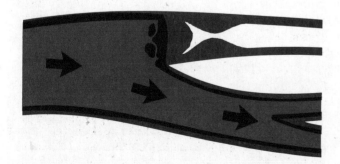

Figure 16. Blood clot lodged in artery of neck or brain, depriving brain tissues of essential oxygen.

Hemorrhage

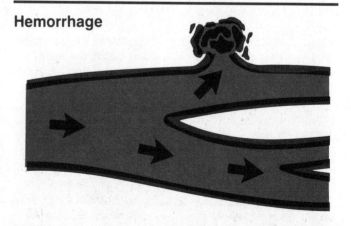

Figure 17. Blood flowing into brain tissue through ruptured arterial walls.

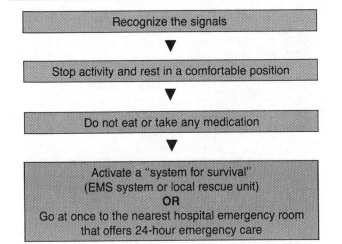

Recognize the signals
▼
Stop activity and rest in a comfortable position
▼
Do not eat or take any medication
▼
Activate a "system for survival" (EMS system or local rescue unit) OR Go at once to the nearest hospital emergency room that offers 24-hour emergency care

Figure 18. Emergency action plan for person with warning signals of stroke.

Actions for Survival: Prevention is the best medicine, and the most important measure for prevention of stroke is the early recognition and treatment of high blood pressure.

If an individual is observed having any of the signals of stroke, have the person stop activity and rest in a comfortable position (Figure 18). No food should be eaten or medication taken. The signals of stroke are not as easy to misinterpret as are those of a heart attack. This seems to lead to easier recognition of the problem by family and friends of the victim than is true for the victim of heart attack. In addition, perhaps because of the alarming nature of the signals, there appears to be less denial on the part of the stroke victim than of someone who suffers a heart attack.

If the signals of stroke persist for 30 seconds and are not otherwise explained, the EMS system should be activated or the victim transported to the nearest hospital offering 24-hour emergency service.

The stroke victim may lose consciousness. If this occurs, the initial steps of CPR must be performed, i.e., the airway must be opened and breathing and circulation evaluated. Most victims will have spontaneous respiration and an adequate pulse, and in these cases the maintenance of a patent airway is all that is required. If respiratory and/or cardiac arrest occurs, then basic life support should be initiated.

American Heart Association publications on stroke include *Strokes: A Guide for the Family* (AHA 50-025-B); *Stroke: Why Do They Behave That Way?* (AHA 50-035-A); *Facts About Strokes* (AHA 51-1001); *Body Language: How Your Body Warns You of an Impending Stroke and What to Do About It* (AHA 51-003-A); *Seven Hopeful Facts About Stroke* (AHA 51-016-C); *Stroke Facts 1987* (AHA 55-035-B) and *Aphasia and the Family* (AHA 50-002-A).

Epilepsy

Epilepsy is a disorder characterized by recurrent seizures that may or may not be convulsive in nature. Epileptic seizures are associated with uncontrolled bursts of brain electrical activity. While there are many causes for epilepsy (such as head trauma), the reason in many persons remains unknown.

Nonconvulsive seizures include 1) staring attacks with loss of awareness for a few seconds, called absence seizures (older term: petit mal) and 2) attacks of confusion and loss of awareness with semipurposeful behavior lasting a few minutes, called complex partial seizures. No first-aid procedures are required for these seizures, but close observation is recommended. Of the convulsive seizures, the generalized tonic clonic or grand mal is the most easily recognized since the person may suddenly fall to the floor and convulse.

Convulsions as a consequence of cardiac arrest can simulate epilepsy. Epileptic seizures are distinguished from those convulsions associated with cardiac arrest by the presence of pulse and blood pressure and by the return of breathing at the termination of the episode. Treatment of a convulsive seizure commonly requires protection of the head, observation during and after the seizure, and at the termination, turning the person to the side to allow pooled secretions to clear. Objects should not be placed in the mouth, and movements should not be restrained. (When available, a "bitestick" may be used if the rescuer is trained to do so.) Aspiration of food may occur as a complication of any seizure and may require treatment as indicated in "Obstructed Airway," Chapter 7. Rarely, sudden death may follow an epileptic seizure and is thought to be secondary to ventricular fibrillation. The same resuscitative measures used for sudden death from coronary heart disease should be followed.

The most important action is to protect the individual. Cradle or place something soft under the victim's head (such as a towel or the rescuer's hands) to prevent head injury. Remove all sharp or dangerous objects that are nearby. Convulsive seizures run their course, and a bystander can do nothing to prevent or terminate an attack. After the seizure, make sure the mouth is cleared of food and saliva by turning the person onto the side. Incontinence (loss of urinary and/or fecal control) is common during a seizure. If the rescuer remains calm, the person will be reassured when alertness is resumed. Do not put liquids into the victim's mouth or offer any food, drink, or medication until the victim is fully awake. (If repeated attacks occur or if the seizure lasts longer than 10 minutes, the individual should be taken immediately to a medical facility.)

Breathing almost always resumes spontaneously after a convulsive seizure. Otherwise, a complication of the seizure has occurred such as the aspiration of food, an associated heart attack, or severe head or neck injury. In this case, CPR should be initiated.

References

1. Boidin MP: Airway patency in the unconscious patient. *Br J Anaesth* 1985;57:306–310.
2. *Accident Facts*, 1984 ed. Chicago, National Safety Council, 1984.
3. *Heart Facts 1987*. Dallas, American Heart Association, 1986.
4. Jenkins CD, Rosenman RH, Zyzanski SJ: Prediction of clinical coronary heart disease by a test for coronary prone behavior pattern. *N Engl J Med* 1974;2901271–1275.
5. *The Health Consequences of Smoking. Cardiovascular Disease*. A Report of the Surgeon General, publication DHHS (PHS) 84-50204. U.S. Department of Health and Human Services, Public Health Service, 1983, ppiv, 127–129.
6. The Lipid Research Clinics Coronary Primary Prevention Trial results. Reduction in incidence of coronary heart disease. Lipid Research Clinics Program. Lipid Metabolism — Atherogenesis Branch, National Heart, Lung, and Blood Institute. *JAMA* 1984;251:351–364.
7. The Lipid Research Clinics Coronary Primary Prevention Trial results. The relationship of reduction in incidence of coronary heart disease to cholesterol lowering. Lipid Research Clinics Program. Lipid Metabolism — Atherogenesis Branch, National Heart:, Lung, and Blood Institute. *JAMA* 1984;251:365–374.
8. Diet in the Healthy Child. Dallas, American Heart Association, 1983.
9. Stamler R, Stamler J, Lindberg HA et al: Asymptomatic hyperglycemia and coronary heart disease in middle-aged men in two employed populations in Chicago. *J Chronic Dis* 1979;32:805–815.
10. Phipps C: Contributory causes of coronary thrombosis. *JAMA* 1936;106:761–762.
11. Master AM, Dack S, Jaffe HL: Factors and events associated with onset of coronary artery thrombosis. *JAMA* 1937;109:546–549.
12. Fitzhugh G, Hamilton BE: Coronary occlusion and fatal angina pectoris: Study of the immediate causes and their prevention. *JAMA* 1933;100:475–480.
13. Smith C, Sauls HC, Ballew J: Coronary occlusion: Clinical study of 100 patients. *Ann Intern Med* 1942;17:681–692.
14. French AJ, Dock W: Fatal coronary arteriosclerosis in young soldiers. *JAMA* 1944;124:1233–1237.
15. Boas EP: Some immediate causes of cardiac infarction. *Am Heart J* 1942;23:1–15.
16. Levine HD: Acute myocardial infarction following wasp sting. Report of two cases and critical survey of the literature. *Am Heart J* 1976;91:365–374.
17. Jenkins CD: Recent evidence supporting psychologic and social risk factors for coronary disease. *N Engl J Med* 1976;294:1033–1038.
18. Rahe RH, Romo M, Bennett L et al: Recent life changes, myocardial infarction, and abrupt coronary death. Studies in Helsinki. *Arch Intern Med* 1974;133:221–228.
19. Thompson RG, Hallstrom AP, Cobb LA: Bystander-initiated cardiopulmonary resuscitation in the management of ventricular fibrillation. *Ann Intern Med* 1979;90:737–740.
20. Lund I, Skulberg A: Cardiopulmonary resuscitation by lay people. *Lancet* 1979;2:702–704.
21. Adgey AA, Pantridge JF: Symposium on arteriosclerotic heart disease. The prehospital phase of treatment for myocardial infarction. *Geriatrics* 1972;27:102–110.
22. Crampton RS, Aldrich R, Stillerman R et al: Reduction of community mortality from coronary artery disease after initiation of prehospital cardiopulmonary resuscitation and emergency cardiac care. National Conference on Standards for Cardiopulmonary Resuscitation (CPR) and Emergency Cardiac Care (ECC):, Washington, DC, 1973, pp 193–195.
23. Eisenberg MS, Bergner L, Hallstrom A: Cardiac resuscitation in the community. Importance of rapid provision and implications for program planning. *JAMA* 1979; 241:1905–1907.
24. Plueckhahn VD: Death by drowning? *Med J Aust* 1975;2:904–906.
25. Siebke H, Rod T, Breivik H, et al: Survival after 40 minutes submersion without cerebral sequelae. *Lancet* 1975;1:1275–1277.
26. Southwick FS, Dalgish PH: Recovery after prolonged asystolic cardiac arrest in profound hypothermia. A case report and literature review. *JAMA* 1980;243:1250–1253.
27. Scholander PF: The master switch of life. *Sci Ami* 1963;209:92–106.
28. Steinman AM: The hypothermic code: CPR controversy revisited. *J Emerg Med Serv* 1983;10:32–35.
29. Steinman AM: The hypothermic code. *J Emerg Med Serv* 1983;8:32–35.
30. *Definitive Studies on Pole-top Resuscitation*. Prepared by Gordon AS, Ridolpho PF, Cole JE, Research Resuscitation Laboratories. Camarillo, Calif., Electric Power Research Institute, 1983.
31. Baker CC, Thomas AN, Trunkey DD: The role of emergency room thoracotomy in trauma. *J Trauma* 1980;20:848–855.
32. Mattox KL, Feliciano DV: Role of external cardiac compression in truncal trauma. *J Trauma* 1982;22:934–936.
33. Vij D, Simoni E, Smith RF, et al: Resuscitative thoracotomy of patients with traumatic injury. *Surgery* 1983;94:554–561.
34. Shimazu S, Shatney CH: Outcomes of trauma patients with no vital signs on hospital admission. *J Trauma* 1983;23:213–216.
35. Cogbill TH, Moore EE, Millikan JS, et al: Rationale for selective application of emergency department thoracotomy in trauma. *J Trauma* 1983;23:453–460.
36. Flynn TC, Ward RE, Miller PW: Emergency department thoracotomy. *Ann Emerg Med* 1982;11:413–416.
37. Kannel WB, Wolf P, Dawber TR: Hypertension and cardiac impairments increase stroke risk. *Geriatrics* 1978;33:71–83.
38. Kannel WB, Wolf PA, Verter J: Manifestations of coronary disease predisposing to stroke. The Framingham study. *JAMA* 1983;250:2942–2946.
39. Beevers DG, Hamilton M, Fairman MJ et al: Antihypertensive treatment and the course of established cerebral vascular disease. *Lancet* 1973;1:1407–1409.
40. Freis ED: The Veterans Administration Cooperative Study on Antihypertensive Agents. Implications for stroke prevention. *Stroke* 1974;5:75–77.
41. McDowall FH: Prevention of subsequent infarctions and transient ischemic attacks. *Adv Neurol* 1979;25:277–286.
42. Dyken ML, Wolf PA, Barnett HJM, et al: Risk factors in stroke. A statement for physicians by the Subcommittee on Factors and Stroke of the Stroke Council. *Stroke* 1984;15:1105–1111.

Chapter 3

Introduction to the Performance of CPR

Basic life support (BLS) is that phase of emergency cardiac care (ECC) that either 1) prevents circulatory or respiratory arrest or insufficiency through prompt recognition and intervention or 2) externally supports, with cardiopulmonary resuscitation (CPR), the circulation and respiration of a victim of cardiac and/or respiratory arrest.[1] The major objective of CPR is to provide oxygen to the heart, brain, and other vital organs until appropriate, definitive medical treatment (ACLS) can restore normal heart action. Speed is critical — the key to success.

The highest hospital discharge rate — a measure of resuscitation success — is achieved in those patients for whom CPR is initiated within 4 minutes of the time of arrest and who, in addition, are provided with ACLS treatment within 8 minutes of their arrest.[2] The victim whose heart and breathing have stopped for less than 4 minutes has an excellent chance for full recovery if CPR is administered immediately. After 4–6 minutes without circulation, brain damage may occur; after 6 minutes, except in unusual circumstances (drowning in cold water, for example), brain damage will almost always occur. For these reasons early bystander CPR intervention and fast EMS response are essential in improving survival rates[3–5] and neurological recovery rates.[6, 7] It is most important to

- Recognize the need for immediate action and, if appropriate,
- Perform the steps of CPR promptly and effectively

Basic life support includes the teaching of primary and secondary prevention. The basic concept, presented by the American Heart Association during the last 20 years, that it is possible to control and may be possible to prevent coronary heart disease,[8] should be reinforced during the teaching of BLS, with emphasis on prudent heart living and the role of risk factor modification. The earlier this information is transmitted to the community, the stronger the impact on mortality and morbidity. Cardiopulmonary resuscitation training should include information on danger signals, actions for survival, and entry into the EMS system in order to help prevent sudden death in individuals who have sustained myocardial infarctions.

Indications for CPR

Respiratory Arrest

When breathing stops first, the heart can continue to pump blood for several minutes, and existing oxygen in the lungs and blood will continue to circulate to the brain and other vital organs. Early intervention in victims in whom respirations stop or the airway is obstructed may prevent cardiac arrest. Some of the conditions that will produce respiratory arrest are drowning, stroke, airway obstruction (choking), smoke inhalation, drug overdose, electrocution, suffocation, physical trauma (as in automobile accidents), and heart attack.

If breathing alone is inadequate or absent, opening the airway, rescue breathing, or both may be all that is necessary.

Cardiac Arrest

When the heart stops, blood is not circulated and oxygen stored in the vital organs will be depleted in a few seconds.

If circulation is also absent, external chest compressions must be started in combination with rescue breathing.

The ABCs of CPR

Understanding the rationale of the sequence of steps in CPR is essential to effective BLS. Cardiopulmonary resuscitation is based on three areas of focus, or three basic skills groups:

Airway,
Breathing, and
Circulation

(the "ABCs of CPR"). At the beginning of each of the ABCs is an assessment phase: **A**irway — **determine unresponsiveness; B**reathing — **determine breathlessness; C**irculation — **determine pulselessness.**

The assessment phases, or steps, of CPR are crucial. No victim should undergo any one of the intrusive interventions of CPR (positioning, opening the airway, finger sweep, rescue breathing, and external chest compressions) until the need for it has been established by the appropriate assessment. Unwarranted interventions may be harmful.

Decisions about performing the steps of CPR should always be based on information gained from performing the assessment phases. (Assessment also involves the more subtle, constant process of observing and interacting with the victim.)

The EMS System

An EMS system is a coordinated, community-wide means of responding to sudden illness or injury. The system involves many elements: trained personnel, communications, transportation, emergency care units, public safety agencies, consumer participation, patient transfer, public information and education, evaluation, disaster linkage, and mutual aid agreements.

Knowing how to obtain access to the EMS system in one's locale is important. Access is usually accomplished by telephone. The ideal access number is 911, which is part of a widely used emergency system; but this system is not in place nationwide. Less desirable is "0" for operator or a specific emergency number. The telephone number in each community should be widely publicized so that every citizen is aware of it. If no telephone is available, seeking help by any means is appropriate.

The rescuer who calls the EMS system should be prepared to give the following information in a calm manner:

1. *Where* the emergency is (with address, names of landmarks, cross-streets, and/or roads, if possible)
2. *Phone number* from which the call is made
3. *What happened* — heart attack, auto accident, etc.
4. *How many persons need help*
5. *Condition of the victim(s)*
6. *What aid is being given* to the victim(s)

Finally, *the rescuer should hang up last.* The other person should acknowledge that all necessary information has been received and should release the caller.

Bystanders trained in CPR should provide immediate rescue procedures, including CPR, until the EMS system or local rescue unit responds. Trained professionals will respond to the call and stabilize the victim for transport to an emergency facility.

Summary

CPR is a basic lifesaving technique focusing on **A**irway, **B**reathing, and **C**irculation to assure an open airway and to support respiration and circulation with rescue breaths and external chest compressions when necessary. Each of the ABCs of CPR begins with an assessment phase. No interventions should be started until the appropriate assessment phase has been carried out. Success in CPR requires immediate recognition and proper action by the bystander and rapid response, with ACLS, from the EMS system. The best way to save lives, though, is through prevention.

Subsequent chapters will include detailed descriptions of the steps of CPR as used in the following BLS sequences:

- One-rescuer CPR
- Two-rescuer CPR
- Foreign body airway obstruction management
- Pediatric resuscitation

References

1. *A Manual for Instructors in Basic Life Support,* Dallas, American Heart Association, 1977.
2. Eisenberg MS, Bergner L, Hallstrom A: Cardiac resuscitation in the community. Importance of rapid provision and implications for program planning. *JAMA* 1979;241:1905–1907.
3. Cobb LA, Werner JA, Trobaugh GB: Sudden cardiac death: Parts 1 and 2. *Mod Concepts Cardiovasc Dis* 1980;49:31–36, 37–42.
4. Eisenberg MS, Copass MK, Hallstrom AP, et al: Treatment of out-of-hospital cardiac arrest with rapid defibrillation by emergency medical technicians. *N Engl J Med* 1980;302:1379–1383.
5. Myerburg RJ, Kessler KM, Zaman L, et al: Survivors of prehospital cardiac arrest. *JAMA* 1982;247:1485–1490.
6. Abramson N, Safar P, Detre K, et al; An international collaborative clinical study mechanism for resuscitation research. *Resuscitation* 1982;10:141–147.
7. Longstreth WT, Diehr P, Inui TS: Prediction of awakening after out-of-hospital cardiac arrest. *N Engl J Med* 1983;308:1378–1382.
8. *Risk Factors and Coronary Disease: A Statement for Physicians.* Dallas, American Heart Association, 1980.

Techniques of CPR

The techniques and principles of CPR are similar whether a rescuer is performing one-rescuer CPR, two-rescuer CPR, pediatric resuscitation, or relief of an obstructed airway. This chapter reviews in detail all of the techniques of CPR; subsequent chapters outline and adapt these CPR techniques to varying rescue situations.

The steps of assessment and the initiation and performance of CPR are discussed fully, with background and rationale information presented when appropriate. The Instructor should be prepared to present this material in detail, use the background and rationale to support the methods presented, and respond to questions.

AIRWAY

The first phase in the ABCs of CPR is Airway.

Assessment: Determine Unresponsiveness

The rescuer arriving at the scene of a collapsed person (victim) must quickly assess for any injury and determine if the individual is unconscious. If the victim has sustained trauma to the head and neck, the rescuer should not move the victim unless it is necessary. Improper movement in the case of a neck injury may cause paralysis. The circumstances in which the victim is found — near a ladder, in a pool, in an auto accident, as opposed to slumped in a chair or on the floor — will give some indication of the possibility or probability of neck injury.

Gently shake the victim and shout, "Are you ok?" (Figure 19). This precaution will help prevent the rescuer from possibly doing injury by attempting to move and/or resuscitate a person who is, for instance, sleeping. The unresponsive victim is likely to be unconscious and need CPR.

Figure 19. Determine unresponsiveness.

Figure 20. Call for help.

Call for Help

If the victim does not respond to attempts at arousal, call out for help (Figure 20). Even if no one is in sight, call out in the hope that someone will hear who can assist or activate the EMS system.

Positioning

Position the Victim

For CPR to be effective, the victim must be horizontal, supine (lying on the back), and on a firm, flat surface; even flawlessly performed external chest compressions will produce no blood flow to the brain if the body is in a vertical position. Blood flow to the brain will be compromised if the head is higher than the feet. Airway management and rescue breathing are also more easily achieved when the patient is supine.

It is imperative to position the unconscious victim as quickly as possible. If the person is lying crumpled or face down, repositioning must take place before CPR is initiated. Particular caution must be exercised if a neck or back injury is suspected.

The victim must be rolled as a unit so that the head, shoulders, and torso move simultaneously — with no twisting (Figure 21). (A neck or spine injury may be complicated by twisting the victim's body.) The rescuer should kneel beside the victim at a distance approximately equal to the width of the victim's body and at the level of the victim's shoulders. This permits sufficient space to roll the victim while the neck is supported. The victim's arm closer to the rescuer should be raised above the victim's head. The victim's legs should be straight or bent slightly at the knees. The rescuer places one hand behind the victim's head and neck (Figure 21) for support. The other hand should grasp the victim under the arm to brace the shoulder and torso. The victim is then rolled toward the rescuer by pulling steadily and evenly at the shoulder while controlling the head and neck. The head and neck should remain in the same plane as the torso, and the body should be moved as a unit.

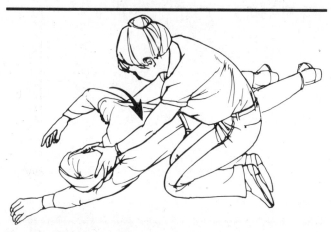

Figure 21. Position the victim.

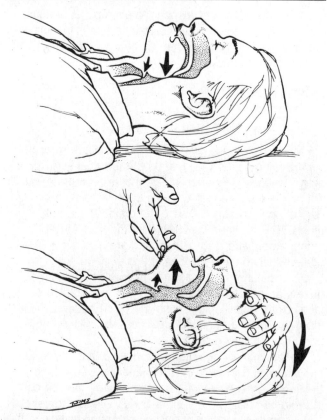

Figure 22. Opening the airway. Top: Airway obstruction produced by the tongue and the epiglottis. Bottom: Relief by head-tilt/chin-lift.

Once the victim is supine, the victim's arms are placed alongside the body. The victim is now appropriately positioned for the next step in CPR.

Rescuer Position

By kneeling at the level of the victim's shoulders, the rescuer can perform rescue breathing and external chest compressions without moving the knees.

Open the Airway

The most important action for successful resuscitation is immediate opening of the airway. In the absence of sufficient muscle tone, the tongue and/or epiglottis will obstruct the pharynx and/or the larynx, respectively (Figure 22, top).[1-5] The tongue is the most common cause of obstruction in the unconscious victim. Since the tongue is attached to the lower jaw, moving the jaw forward will lift the tongue and the epiglottis away from the back of the throat and open the airway (Figure 22, bottom). Also, either the tongue or the epiglottis,[5] or both, may produce obstruction when negative pressure is created in the airway by inspiratory effort, causing a valve-type mechanism to occlude the entrance to the trachea. Opening the airway may be all that is needed to relieve the obstruction and allow the victim to breathe.

The rescuer should use the head-tilt/chin-lift maneuver, described below, to open the airway. If foreign material or vomitus is visible in the mouth, it should be removed. Excessive time must not be taken. Liquids or semiliquids should be wiped out with the index and middle fingers covered by a piece of cloth; solid material should be extracted with a hooked index finger. The mouth can be opened by the "crossed-finger" technique.[6]

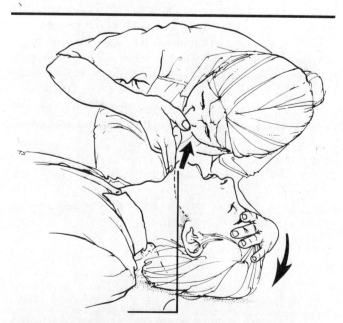

Figure 23. Head-tilt/chin-lift maneuver. Perpendicular line reflects proper neck extension, i.e., a line along the edge of the jaw bone should be perpendicular to the surface on which the victim is lying.

Head-Tilt/Chin-Lift

Head-tilt/chin-lift is recommended for opening the airway.[7] Head-tilt is accomplished by placing one hand on the victim's forehead and applying firm, backward pressure with the palm to tilt the head back (Figure 23). To complete the head-tilt/chin-lift maneuver, place the fingers of the other hand under the bony part of the lower jaw near the chin and lift to bring the chin forward and the teeth almost to occlusion, thus supporting the jaw and helping to tilt the head back. The fingers must not press deeply into the soft tissue under the chin, which might obstruct the airway. The thumb should not be used for lifting the chin. The mouth should not be completely closed (unless mouth-to-nose breathing is the technique of choice for that particular victim). When mouth-to-nose ventilation is indicated, the hand that is already on the chin can close the mouth by applying increased force and, in this way, provide effective mouth-to-nose ventilation.[4] If the victim has loose dentures, head-tilt/chin-lift maintains their position and makes a mouth-to-mouth seal easier.[7] Dentures should be removed if they cannot be managed in place.

Jaw-Thrust

Additional forward displacement of the jaw by use of the jaw-thrust maneuver may be required. This can be accomplished by grasping the angles of the victim's lower jaw and lifting with both hands, one on each side, displacing the mandible forward while tilting the head backward (Figure 24).[6, 8] The rescuer's elbows should rest on the surface on which the victim is lying. If the lips close, the lower lip can be retracted with the thumb. If mouth-to-mouth breathing is necessary, the nostrils may be closed by placing the rescuer's cheek tightly against them.[6]

Jaw-thrust (or chin-lift), without head-tilt, is the safest first approach to opening the airway of the victim with a suspected neck injury because it usually can be accomplished without extending the neck. The head should be carefully supported without tilting it backward or turning it from side to side. If this maneuver is unsuccessful, the head should be tilted backward very slightly.

Figure 24. Jaw-thrust maneuver.

Background on Airway Opening Techniques

Since head-tilt/neck-lift was recommended in the past, the following background information is provided to help the Instructor answer possible questions on opening the airway.

In 1960 Elam et al[9] described the technique for head-tilt/chin-lift as follows:

> Mouth-to-mouth and mouth-to-nose methods of artificial respiration are simplified and made more effective if the patient's neck is extended by the procedure here described. With the patient in the supine or semilateral position, the rescuer uses one hand to tilt the patient's head as far back as possible. He uses his other hand to pull the patient's chin upward. Circumstances determine whether the rescuer will apply his mouth to the mouth or the nose of the patient.

There was no indication in the article that the hand lifting the neck was to remain there. Its only use was in the initial tilting of the head; that hand was then removed and used to support the chin. (Neck-lift may not be needed to establish head-tilt. Lifting the chin and tilting the head may open the airway and accomplish the result more easily.) Again, in Ruben et al[10] head-tilt/neck-lift was used only in the initial maneuver for tilting the head backward, not for opening or maintaining the airway or for mouth-to-mouth rescue breathing. Greene et al[11] stated: "When hyperextension of the head (50°) was produced by lifting the chin as well as pushing backward at the vertex or frontal region, a wider air passage uniformly appeared."

A study by Guildner[7] begun in the late 1960's recorded the adequacy of three techniques for opening an airway obstructed by the tongue. The study reported the effectiveness of neck-lift, chin-lift, and jaw-thrust, when combined with head-tilt, in producing an adequate tidal volume. The adequacy of ventilation was compared subjectively and by measuring airflow. Results of the study indicated that chin-lift provided the most consistently adequate airway. Points of particular note in this study include the following:

- Head-tilt/chin-lift consistently provided a more effective method of opening the airway in the unconscious victims who were not breathing or who were making spontaneous respiratory efforts.
- Both neck-lift and jaw-thrust were consistently more tiring than head-tilt/chin-lift.
- Patients with loose dentures posed a serious problem to mouth-to-mouth rescue breathing, as they frequently caused a worsened airway obstruction when mouth-to-mouth contact was made for rescue breathing using the head-tilt/neck-lift technique. Head-tilt/chin-lift, however, by supporting the lower jaw and bringing the teeth almost to occlusion, maintains the position of loose dentures and makes a mouth-to-mouth seal easier and more effective.

In 1979, at the request of the AHA Committee on Emergency Cardiac Care, the American Society of Anesthesiologists contacted 30 anesthesiologists, all actively involved in teaching CPR, and asked them to review the literature, assess current practices of emergency airway management, and make recommendations. The overwhelming consensus was that it seemed appropriate to adopt head-tilt/chin-lift as the preferred technique for opening the airway. Head-tilt/neck-lift offers no advantage over head-tilt/chin-lift.

A layperson should learn only one maneuver for opening the airway. The recommended technique must be simple, safe, easily learned, and effective. Since head-tilt/chin-lift meets these criteria, it is the method of choice. Healthcare providers (RNs, EMTs, MDs, etc.) should be trained in both head-tilt/chin-lift and jaw-thrust.

BREATHING

The second phase of the ABCs of CPR is Breathing.

Assessment: Determine Breathlessness

To assess the presence or absence of spontaneous breathing in a victim, the rescuer's ear should be placed over the victim's mouth and nose while maintaining an open airway position. Then, while observing the victim's chest, the rescuer should

- LOOK for the chest to rise and fall
- LISTEN for air escaping during exhalation and
- FEEL for the flow of air

If the chest does not rise and fall and no air is exhaled, the victim is breathless. This assessment should take only 3–5 seconds. If breathlessness is diagnosed, the next step must be instituted.

Rescue Breathing

All individuals participating in a BLS Healthcare Provider's Course (Course C) **must be trained in the use of a mask** with a one-way valve for instruction in rescue breathing. Students should be provided with a mask with a one-way valve, or the valve alone, which can be inserted into a clean mask. Mouth-to-mask rescue breathing technique is described in detail in Chapter 9, "Special Techniques."

Mouth-to-Mouth

Rescue breathing by mouth-to-mouth ventilation is the quickest, most effective means of providing the necessary oxygen to the victim's lungs. The rescuer's exhaled air contains sufficient oxygen to supply the victim's needs. Rescue breathing requires that the rescuer inflate the victim's lungs adequately with each breath. The rescuer must be able to tell if the technique is correct. (Is air getting into the lungs or is an airway obstruction preventing the free flow of air?) The rescuer must maintain the airway and create an airtight seal when breathing for the victim.

To preserve an open airway the rescuer should be positioned by the victim's shoulders as in opening the airway. Head-tilt/chin-lift must be maintained throughout the rescue breathing procedure. Efforts to breathe for the victim will be useless if the tongue and/or epiglottis block the airway.

The first part of the airtight seal is the nose pinch, which seals the nostrils and prevents air escaping through the nose. The thumb and index finger of the hand maintaining head-tilt should be used to gently pinch the nostrils closed. The rescuer should take a deep breath, seal the lips around the outside of the victim's mouth, creating an airtight seal, and give two full breaths — air is blown into the victim's mouth while watching for the chest to rise (Figure 25).

Adequate time for the two breaths (1–1.5 sec/inflation) should be allowed to provide good chest expansion and decrease the possibility of gastric distention. The rescuer should take a breath after each ventilation, and each individual ventilation should be of sufficient volume to make the chest rise. In most adults, this volume will be 800 mL (0.8 L). Adequate ventilation usually does not need to exceed 1,200 mL (1.2 L). An excess of air volume and fast inspiratory flow rates are likely to cause pharyngeal pressures that exceed esophageal opening pressures, allowing air to enter the stomach and, thus, resulting in gastric distention.[12–14] ("Four quick" breaths were recommended formerly. By giving two ventilations with a slower inspiratory flow rate and by avoiding trapping air in the lungs between breaths, the possibility of exceeding the esophageal opening pressure will be less.) Indicators of adequate ventilation are 1) observing the chest rise and fall and 2) hearing and feeling the air escape during exhalation.

If the initial attempt to ventilate the victim is unsuccessful, the rescuer should reposition the victim's head and repeat rescue breathing. Improper chin and head positioning is the most common cause of difficulty with ventilation. If the victim cannot be ventilated after repositioning the head, the rescuer should proceed with foreign body airway obstruction management procedures (see Chapter 7).

Mouth-to-Nose

This technique (Figure 26) is more effective in some cases than mouth-to-mouth rescue breathing.[15] The technique is recommended when it is impossible to ventilate through the victim's mouth, the mouth cannot be opened (trismus), the mouth is seriously injured, or a tight mouth-to-mouth seal is difficult to achieve. The rescuer should keep the victim's head tilted back with one hand on the forehead and use the other hand to lift the victim's lower jaw (as in head-tilt/chin-lift) and close the mouth. The rescuer should then take a deep breath, seal the lips around the victim's nose, and blow into the nose. The rescuer should then remove his or her mouth as the victim exhales passively. It may be necessary to open the victim's mouth intermittently or separate the lips (with the thumb) to allow air to be exhaled since nasal obstruction may be present during exhalation.[16]

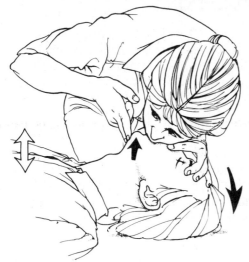

Figure 25. Mouth-to-mouth rescue breathing.

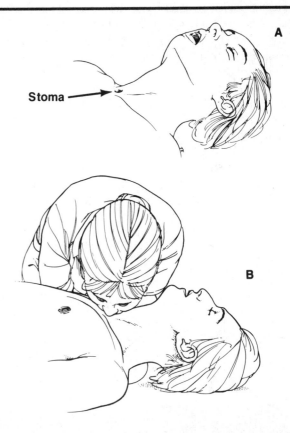

Figure 27. (A) Anatomy of a permanent stoma. (B) Mouth-to-stoma rescue breathing. (Adapted from *Cardiopulmonary Resuscitation*, Washington, D.C., American Red Cross, 1987, pp. 16, 17. Used by permission.)

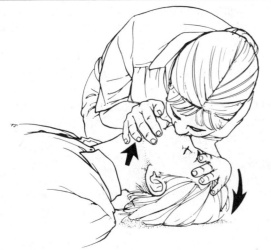

Figure 26. Mouth-to-nose breathing.

Mouth-to-Stoma[17]

Persons who have undergone a laryngectomy (surgical removal of the larynx) have a permanent stoma (opening) that connects the trachea directly to the skin. The stoma can be recognized as an opening at the front base of the neck. When such an individual requires rescue breathing, direct mouth-to-stoma ventilation should be performed (Figure 27). The assessment for breathing is done at the base of the neck, where the stoma is located (Figure 28). The rescuer's mouth is sealed around the stoma, and air is blown into it until the chest rises. When the rescuer's mouth is removed from the stoma, the victim is permitted to exhale passively.

Other persons may have a temporary tracheostomy tube in the trachea. To ventilate these persons, the victim's mouth and nose usually must be sealed by the rescuer's hand or by a tightly fitting face mask to prevent leakage of air when the rescuer blows into the tracheostomy tube. This problem is alleviated when the tracheostomy tube has a cuff that can be inflated.

Figure 28. Assessing respirations at the stoma.

Complications

Inadequate and excessive ventilations and complications of rescue breathing (gastric distention) are discussed in Chapter 9.

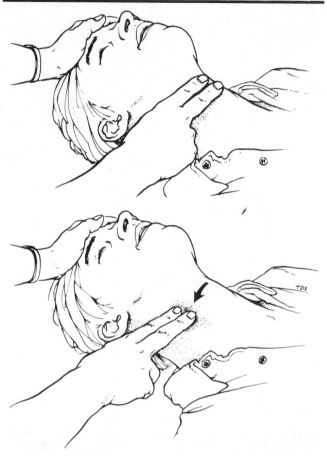

Figure 29. Locating the carotid pulse.

CIRCULATION

All of the ABCs of BLS are required to adequately treat a victim of cardiac arrest. **A**irway and **B**reathing have been discussed; the third phase is **C**irculation. Cardiac arrest is recognized by pulselessness in the large arteries of the unconscious, breathless victim.

Assessment: Determine Pulselessness

If the rescuer has successfully given two breaths and observes the victim's chest rise, a check for the presence or absence of pulse must be performed. The inability to find a palpable pulse will establish the diagnosis of cardiac arrest and the need for external chest compressions.

Locate the Carotid Pulse

The neck or carotid pulse lies in a groove created by the windpipe and the large strap muscles of the neck. It is the most accessible, most reliable, and most easily learned method for adults and children. The rescuer is already at the location of the carotid artery; and further, the carotid arteries are closer to the heart, and sometimes these pulses will persist when more peripheral (arm) pulses are no longer palpable. All basic rescuers are instructed in finding the carotid pulse and should practice during class. For healthcare providers, or in the hospital setting, determining pulselessness with the femoral pulse is also acceptable; however, this pulse is difficult to locate in a fully clothed patient.

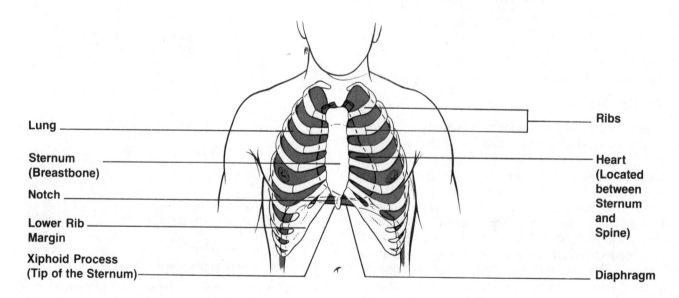

Lung

Sternum (Breastbone)

Notch

Lower Rib Margin

Xiphoid Process (Tip of the Sternum)

Ribs

Heart (Located between Sternum and Spine)

Diaphragm

Figure 30. Location of body landmarks.

While maintaining head-tilt with one hand on the forehead, the rescuer should locate the victim's thyroid cartilage (Adam's apple) with two or three fingers of the other hand. The rescuer then should slide these fingers into the groove between the trachea and the muscles at the side of the neck where the carotid pulse can be felt. The pulse area must be probed gently, avoiding compression of the artery, and should be felt on only one side, usually that nearer the rescuer (Figure 29).

The disadvantages of palpating the pulse on the opposite side are as follows:

1. The windpipe interferes with palpation.
2. The windpipe may be compressed, obstructing the airway and reversing the head-tilt position,
3. A tendency to feel with the fingers on the far side and the thumb on the near side causes bilateral pressure, and a carotid sinus reflex can be stimulated, slowing the heart rate,
4. Reaching across causes difficulties in locating the groove, and the rescuer tends to try to palpate the carotid artery through the strap muscle,
5. Simultaneous palpation of both carotids can obstruct blood flow to the brain.

If There Is a Pulse

Locating and palpating a pulse will take 5–10 seconds. It takes time to find the correct location, and the pulse may be slow, irregular, or very weak and rapid.

Performing CPR on a patient who has a pulse may result in serious medical complications; be sure to properly assess the victim's condition. If a pulse is present but there is no breathing, rescue breathing should be initiated at a rate of 12 times/minute, or once every 5 seconds (after the initial two breaths of 1–1.5 seconds each).

If There Is No Pulse

If no pulse is palpated, the diagnosis of cardiac arrest is confirmed. At this point, if the EMS system has not already been activated, it should be now; and external chest compressions should be begun.

Activate the EMS System

If the rescuer is not alone, one person should be sent to call the local emergency telephone number, activating the EMS system if not previously done. As discussed earlier, the shorter the intervals between collapse, initiation of basic CPR, and advanced cardiac life support, the more likely the survival of the cardiac arrest victim. If the rescuer is alone, CPR should be performed for 1 minute and then help summoned. The decision when to leave the victim and make the telephone call is affected by a number of variables, including the possibility that someone else may arrive on the scene. If the rescuer is unable to activate the EMS system, the only option is to continue CPR.

Perform External Chest Compressions

External chest compressions provide circulation to the heart, lungs, brain, and rest of the body as a result of a generalized increase in pressure within the thoracic cavity as well as direct compression of the heart. Blood circulated to the lungs by external chest compressions will pick up oxygen necessary to maintain life. Nevertheless, artificial circulation is not as effective as normal circulation; it generates only about 20% to 30% of the normal output of the heart. (See also "Physiology of Circulation" in this chapter.)

Body Landmarks

The rescuer must be able to locate the following surface markers to perform external chest compressions with an acceptable hand position (Figure 30):

- Lower rib margins
- Notch (where the ribs meet the sternum). Although not a proper anatomic term for this location, *notch* is used to designate a reference point for external chest compressions
- Sternum (breastbone)
- Ribs

If the rescuer cannot locate the landmarks, sufficient clothing should be removed to permit proper positioning for external chest compressions. All rescuers should understand the relative location of the diaphragm, heart, lungs, liver, and spleen (see Chapter 2).

Proper Hand Position

Proper hand placement is established by the following guidelines:

1. With the middle and index fingers of the hand nearer the patient's legs, the rescuer locates the lower margin of the victim's rib cage on the side next to the rescuer (Figure 31).

Figure 31. External chest compressions: locating the rib margin.

2. The fingers are then run up the rib cage to the notch where the ribs meet the sternum in the center of the lower chest (Figure 32).

3. With the middle finger on this notch, the index finger is placed next to the middle finger on the lower end of the sternum (Figure 32).

4. The heel of the hand nearer the patient's head (which had been used on the forehead to maintain head-tilt) is placed on the lower half of the sternum, close to the index finger that is next to the middle finger that located the notch. The long axis of the heel of the rescuer's hand should be placed on the long axis of the sternum. This will keep the main line of the force of compression on the sternum and decrease the chance of rib fracture (Figure 33).

5. The first hand is then removed from the notch, placed on top of the hand on the sternum so that both hands are parallel, and directed straight away from the rescuer.

6. The fingers may be either extended or interlaced but must be kept off the chest (Figure 34).

7. Because of the varying sizes and shapes of different persons' hands, an alternate acceptable hand position is suggested. It is to grasp the wrist of the hand on the chest with the hand that has been locating the lower end of the sternum. This technique is helpful for rescuers with arthritic problems of the hands and wrists.

Proper Compression Techniques

Effective compression is accomplished by attention to the following guidelines:

1. The elbows are locked into position, the arms are straightened, and the shoulders of the rescuer are positioned directly over the hands so that the thrusts of external chest compressions are straight down on the sternum. If the thrusts are other than straight down, the torso has a tendency to roll, part of the force is lost, and the chest compressions may be less effective (Figure 35).

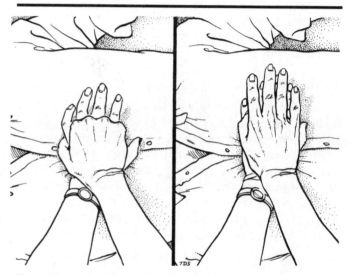

Figure 34. Hand positions for external chest compressions.

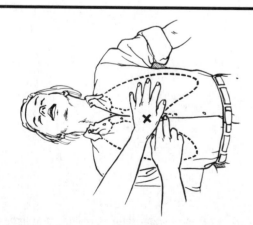

Figure 32. External chest compressions: locating the notch where the rib margin meets the sternum.

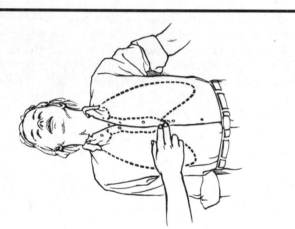

Figure 33. External chest compressions: locating the correct hand position on the lower half of the sternum.

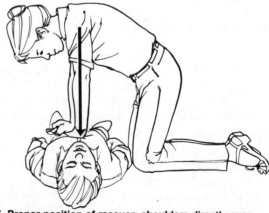

Figure 35. Proper position of rescuer: shoulders directly over victim's sternum; elbows locked. (Adapted from *Cardiopulmonary Resuscitation,* Washington, DC, American Red Cross, 1981, p 25. Used by permission.)

2. To achieve the most pressure with the least effort, the rescuer leans forward until his or her shoulders are directly over his or her outstretched hands (that is, leans forward until the body reaches natural imbalance — a point at which there would be a sensation of falling forward if the hands and arms were not providing support). The weight of the rescuer's back creates the necessary pressure that makes compressions easier on the arms and shoulders. Natural body weight falling forward provides the force to depress the sternum.

3. The sternum must be depressed 1½–2 inches (3.8–5.0 cm) for the normal-size adult (Figure 36).

4. The external chest compression pressure is released to allow blood to flow into the heart (Figure 36). The pressure must be released completely and the chest allowed to return to normal position after each compression. The time allowed for release should equal the time required for compression. Do not pause between compressions.

5. The hands should not be lifted from the chest nor the position changed in any way; otherwise, correct hand position may be lost.

6. An alternate method is sometimes used by small individuals to help provide rhythmic compressions. The rescuer assumes the position previously described but tilts the pelvis forward on the downstroke of each compression and backward on the upstroke of each compression, essentially lifting the knees from the floor.

Bouncing compressions, jerky movements, improper hand position, and leaning on the chest can decrease the effectiveness of resuscitation and are more likely to cause injuries.

Rescue breathing and chest compressons must be combined for effective resuscitation of the cardiopulmonary arrest victim. One- and two-rescuer sequences will be discussed in subsequent chapters.

The external chest compression rate should be a minimum of 80 per minute, and 100 per minute if possible. This rate is consistent with both the "cardiac pump" theory and the "thoracic pump" theory (see below). If the direct compression of the heart is operative, it is clear that a faster rate will increase blood flow. If the increase in intrathoracic pressure is the mechanism of blood flow during CPR, compression with high force and a duration of 50% of cycle time will increase flow to the brain and the heart. A higher compression force and the 50% compression duration is very difficult to obtain with a compression rate of 60 per minute, as was previously recommended. With the compression rate increased, the result is an optimal compression relaxation duration. A faster compression rate also allows for a pause for ventilations in two-rescuer CPR.

Physiology of Circulation

"Closed-Chest Cardiac Massage" was published in 1960.[18] Soon after that this technique was well accepted by professional people and, later, laypersons. It became known as "standard" or "conventional" CPR.

It was believed that external chest compressions resulted in the direct compression of the heart between the sternum and the spine, with an increase in pressure within the ventricles and a closure of the valves (mitral and tricuspid). This pressure was thought to cause blood to move into the pulmonary artery (lungs) and the aorta (blood flow to the organs).

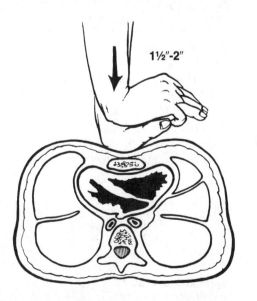
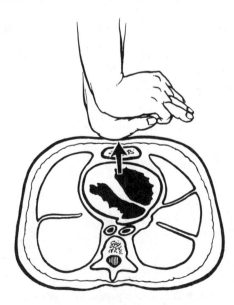

Figure 36. External chest compressions: sternum compressed to a depth of 1½–2 inches (3.8–5.0 cm). Compression-relaxation duration must be 50:50 for better flow to occur.

In support of this "cardiac pump theory"[19] are the studies that demonstrate higher stroke volume and coronary blood flow with high impulse (moderate force and brief duration) external chest compressions at high rates.[20] Preliminary studies reported that there is valve motion and cardiac chamber compression during the initial 5 minutes of external chest compressions.[21]

This conventional theory of blood flow during CPR has been challenged by several workers who have advanced the "thoracic pump mechanism."[22, 23] According to this theory, external chest compressions produce a rise in the intrathoracic pressure that is transmitted equally to all intrathoracic vascular structures. Because arteries resist collapse, there is nearly full transmission of pressure from intrathoracic to extrathoracic arteries (Figure 37). Competent venous valves and venous collapse prevent full transmission of pressure to extrathoracic veins. An extrathoracic arterial-venous pressure gradient is produced that causes blood to flow. This thoracic pump theory is supported by the following observations:

a. In patients with flail chests and who need CPR, the arterial pressure does not increase during chest compressions unless the chest is stabilized with a belt, which allows an increase in intrathoracic pressure.[23]

b. It has been observed that some patients who arrest and are asked to cough vigorously before loss of consciousness are able to remain conscious and that the systolic arterial pressure during coughing is higher than 100 mm Hg. This significant increase in intrathoracic pressure provides blood flow to the brain.[24] The increase in intrathoracic pressure during coughing results from the contraction of the diaphragm, intercostal, and abdominal muscles against a closed glottis.

c. Two-dimensional echocardiography shows that mitral and tricuspid valves remain open during CPR,[25] supporting the concept that the heart is a passive conduit rather than a pump.

It is possible that both mechanisms for blood flow play a role during external chest compressions. Which one is predominant in a particular victim may depend on several factors, including the size of the heart, ventral–dorsal chest diameter, compliance of the chest wall, the magnitude of chest compressions, and perhaps others that are unknown.

Recently, there has been important research in new techniques to improve blood flow during CPR:

1. Simultaneous chest compressions and ventilation (SCV-CPR)[26]
2. Abdominal compression with synchronized ventilation[27]
3. "MAST"-augmented CPR[28]
4. Interposed abdominal compression (IAC-CPR)[29]
5. Continuous abdominal binding[30]

Because many of the proposed techniques require the use of devices (endotracheal intubation, binders, trousers, mechanical compressors, etc.), they cannot be recommended as BLS techniques. Additionally, more information regarding survival rates, neurological outcome, and complications is needed before changes in the technique of external chest compressions are recommended.

Cough CPR

Self-induced CPR is possible; however, its applications are limited to clinical situations in which the patient has a cardiac monitor, the arrest was recognized before loss of consciousness (usually within 10–15 seconds from the cardiac arrest), and the patient has the ability to cough forcefully. The increase in intrathoracic pressure will generate blood flow to the brain to maintain consciousness for a longer period of time.[31]

Summary

Effective resuscitation depends on proper assessment of the victim, followed by appropriate airway, breathing and circulation maneuvers. Care must be taken to follow the proper sequence and performance of CPR procedures, according to established techniques, to provide adequate and safe resuscitation.

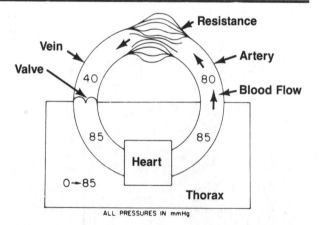

ALL PRESSURES IN mmHg

Figure 37. Effect of increasing intrathoracic pressure on extrathoracic vessels. (Adapted and used by permission of *Annual Review of Medicine* 32:437, 1983. ©1983 by Annual Reviews Inc.)

References

1. Safar P: Ventilatory efficacy of mouth-to-mouth artificial respiration. Airway obstruction during manual and mouth-to-mouth artificial respiration. *JAMA* 1958;167:335–341.
2. Safar P, Escarraga L, Change F: A study of upper airway obstruction in the unconscious patient. *J Appl Physiol* 1959;14:760–764.
3. Morikawa S, Safar P, DeCarlo J: Influence of head position upon upper airway patency. *Anesthesiology* 1961;22:265.
4. Ruben H, Elam JO, Ruben AM, et al: Investigation of upper airway problems in resuscitation. *Anesthesiology* 1961;22:271–279.
5. Boidin MP: Airway patency in the unconscious patient. *Br J Anaesth* 1985;57:306–310.
6. Safar P: *Cardiopulmonary Cerebral Resuscitation.* Stavanger, Norway, Laerdal Co. Philadelphia, WB Saunders Co, 1981.
7. Guildner CW: Resuscitation — opening the airway: A comparative study of techniques for opening an airway obstructed by the tongue. *JACEP* 1976;5:588–590.
8. Esmarch F: *The Surgeon's Handbook.* London, Sampson, Low, Marston, Searle and Rivington, 1878, pp 114–118.
9. Elam JO, Greene DG, Schneider MA, et al: Head tilt method of oral resuscitation. *JAMA* 1960;172:812–815.
10. Ruben HM, Elam JO, Ruben AM et al: Investigation of upper airway problems in resuscitation. 1. Studies of pharyngeal x-rays and performance by laymen. *Anesthesiology* 22:1961;271–279.
11. Greene DG, Elam JO, Dobkin AB, et al: Cinefluorographic study of hyperextension of the neck and upper airway patency. *JAMA* 1961;176:570–573.
12. Ruben H, Knudsen EJ, Carugati G: Gastric inflation in relation to airway pressure. *Acta Anaesth Scand* 1961;5:107–114.
13. Melker R: Asynchronous and other alternative methods of ventilation during CPR. *Ann Emerg Med* 1984;13(pt 2):758–761.
14. Melker R: Recommendations for ventilation during cardiopulmonary resuscitation. Time for change? *Crit Care Med* 1985;13: 882, 883.
15. Ruben H: The immediate treatment of respiratory failure. *Br J Anaesth* 1964;36:542–549.
16. Safar P, Redding J: "Tight jaw" in resuscitation. *Anesthesiology* 1959;20:701–702.
17. *First Aid for (Neck Breathers) Laryngectomees.* International Association of Laryngectomees, New York, NY, American Cancer Society, 1971.
18. Kouwenhoven WB, Jude JR, Knickerbocker GG: Closed-chest cardiac massage. *JAMA* 1960;173:1064–1067.
19. Babbs CF: New versus old theories of blood flow during CPR. *Crit Care Med* 1980;8:191–195.
20. Maier GW, Tyson GS, Olsen CO, et al: The physiology of external cardiac massage: High impulse cardiopulmonary resuscitation. *Circulation* 1984;70:86–101.
21. Deshmukh H, Weil MH, Swindall A, et al: Echocardiographic observations during cardiopulmonary resuscitation: A preliminary report. *Crit Care Med* 1985;13:904–906.
22. Niemann JT, Garner D, Rosborough J, et al: The mechanism of blood flow in closed chest cardiopulmonary resuscitation, abstracted. *Circulation* 1979;60(suppl 2):74.
23. Rudikoff MT, Maughan WL, Effron M, et al: Mechanism of blood flow during cardiopulmonary resuscitation. *Circulation* 1980;61:345–352.
24. Criley JM, Blaufuss AH, Kissel GL: Cough-induced cardiac compression. Self-induced form of cardiopulmonary resuscitation. *JAMA* 1976;236:1246–1250.
25. Werner JA, Greene HL, Janko CL, et al: Visualization of cardiac valve motion during external chest compression using two-dimensional echocardiography. Implications regarding the mechanism of blood flow. *Circulation* 1981;63:1417.
26. Chandra N, Rudikoff M, Weisfelt M: Simultaneous chest compression and ventilation at high airway pressure during cardiopulmonary resuscitation *Lancet* 1980;1:175–178.
27. Rosborough JP, Niemann JT, Criley JM, et al: Lower abdominal compression with synchronized ventilation — a CPR modality. *Circulation* 1981;64:303.
28. Bircher N, Safar P, Steward R: A comparison of standard, "MAST"-augmented, and open-chest CPR in dogs. A preliminary investigation. *Crit Care Med* 1980;8:147–152.
29. Ralston SH, Babbs CF, Niebauer MJ: Cardiopulmonary resuscitation with interposed abdominal compression in dogs. *Anesth Analg* 1982;61:645–651.
30. Niemann JT, Rosborough JP, Ung S, et al: Hemodynamic effects of continuous abdominal binding during cardiac arrest and resuscitation. *Am J Cardiol* 1984;53:269–274.
31. Niemann JT, Rosborough J, Hausknecht M, et al: Cough CPR. Documentation of systemic perfusion in man and in an experimental model: A "window" to the mechanism of blood flow in external CPR. *Crit Care Med* 1980;8:141–146.

A layperson should learn only one-rescuer CPR. The two-rescuer technique is thought to cause too much confusion and to be infrequently used by laypersons in actual rescue situations. One-rescuer CPR is effective in maintaining adequate circulation and ventilation and should be learned by healthcare providers as well, but it is more exhausting than two-rescuer CPR. When two or more trained healthcare providers arrive at the scene of an emergency, they should proceed with two-rescuer CPR and advanced cardiac life support, as appropriate for the situation. The lay rescuer will most likely be relieved of responsibility at this point.

Sequence of Steps for Adult One-Rescuer CPR

The rescuer should be able to perform the following sequence:

AIRWAY

Assessment: Determine unresponsiveness (tap or gently shake and shout).

Call for help.

Position the victim (and assume proper rescuer position).

Open the airway with head-tilt/chin-lift.

BREATHING

Assessment: Determine breathlessness.

If victim is breathing:

- Monitor breathing.
- Maintain open airway.
- Activate the EMS system (if not done previously).

If victim is not breathing:

- Perform rescue breathing by giving two initial breaths.

If unable to give two breaths:

- Reposition head and attempt to ventilate again.
- If still unsuccessful, perform foreign body airway obstruction sequence.

If successful, continue to the next step.

CIRCULATION

Assessment: Determine pulselessness:

- If pulse is present, continue rescue breathing at 12 times/min (once every 5 seconds) and activate the EMS system.
- If pulse is absent, activate the EMS system (if not previously done) and continue to the next step.

Begin external chest compressions: Locate proper hand position. Perform

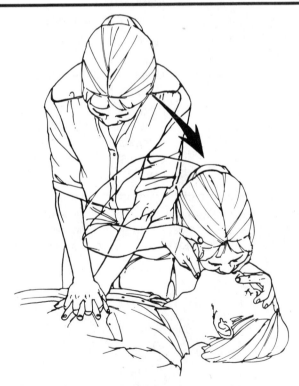

Figure 38. One-rescuer adult CPR. Fifteen compressions are alternated with two ventilations.

15 chest compressions at a rate of 80–100 per minute. Count "one and, two and, three and, four and, five and, six and, seven and, eight and, nine and, ten and, eleven and, twelve and, thirteen and, fourteen and, fifteen."

Open the airway and deliver two rescue breaths within 7 seconds maximum including travel from the compression position to the mouth-to-mouth position.

Locate the proper hand position and begin 15 more compressions at a rate of 80–100 per minute.

Perform four complete cycles of 15 compressions with 2 ventilations (Figure 38).

Reassessment

After four cycles of compressions and ventilations (15:2 ratio), reevaluate the patient:

- Check for return of the carotid pulse.

  If absent:
  Resume CPR with two ventilations followed by compressions.

  If present:
  Continue to the next step.

- Check for breathing.

  If present:
  Monitor breathing and pulse closely.

  If absent:
  Perform rescue breathing at 12 times per minute (once every 5 seconds), and monitor pulse closely.

If CPR is continued, stop and check for return of pulse and spontaneous breathing every few minutes. **Do not interrupt CPR for more than 7 seconds except for special circumstances.**

One-Rescuer CPR with Entry of a Second Rescuer

When another rescuer is available at the scene, it is recommended that this second rescuer activate the EMS (if not done previously) and perform one-rescuer CPR when the first rescuer, who initiated CPR, becomes fatigued.

The following steps are recommended for entry of the second rescuer. The second person identifies him- or herself as a qualified rescuer who is willing to help. If the first rescuer is fatigued and has requested help, the logical sequence is as follows:

1. First rescuer stops CPR after 2 ventilations.
2. Second rescuer kneels down and checks for pulse for 5 seconds.
3. If no pulse, second rescuer gives 2 breaths.
4. Second rescuer commences external chest compressions at the recommended rate and ratio for one-person CPR.
5. First rescuer should assess the adequacy of the second rescuer's ventilations and compressions. This can be done by watching the chest rise during rescue breathing and by checking the pulse during the chest compressions.

Summary: The One-Rescuer Decision Tree

The one-rescuer CPR decision tree (next page) is a review of all the steps for one-rescuer cardiopulmonary resuscitation for the unconscious adult victim.

One-Rescuer CPR Decision Tree

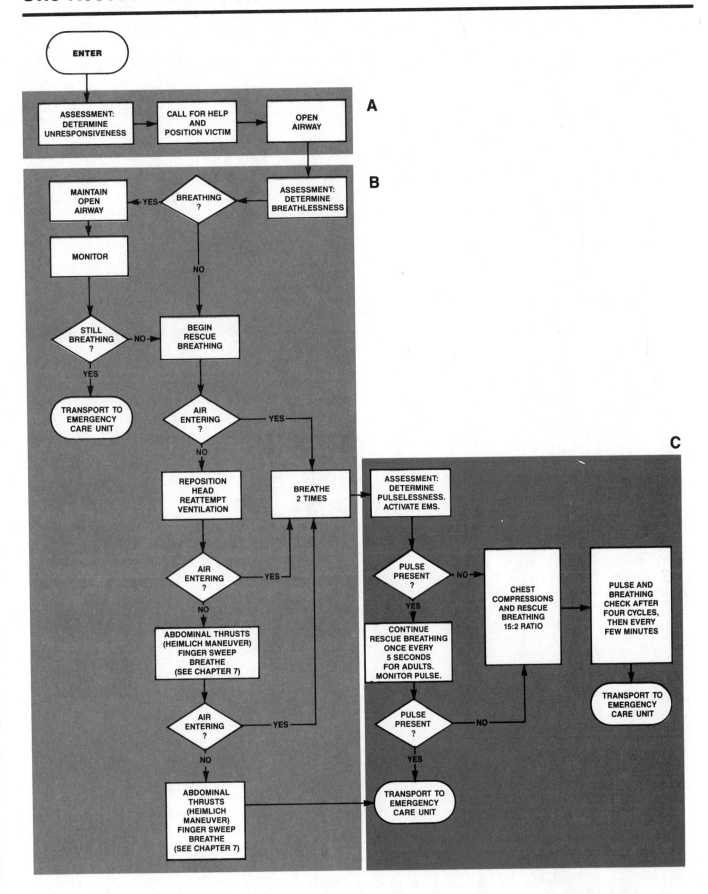

49

All healthcare providers (emergency medicine technicians, physicians, nurses, etc.) should learn both the one-rescuer and the two-rescuer techniques. The latter is less fatiguing. In the two-rescuer coordinated technique for two healthcare providers, mouth-to-mask ventilation is an acceptable alternative for rescue breathing (see Chapter 9).

Advantages of Two-Rescuer CPR

Since artificial circulation must be combined with artificial ventilation, it is preferable to have two rescuers. One rescuer, positioned at the victim's side, performs external chest compressions while the other rescuer, positioned at the victim's head, maintains an open airway and performs ventilations. The compression rate for two-rescuer CPR, as for one-rescuer CPR, is 80–100 per minute. When performed in two-rescuer CPR without interruptions, this rate can maintain adequate blood flow and pressure, reduce rescuer fatigue, and provide for more ventilations. For adequate ventilation, a pause for a rescue breath should be allowed after each 5th compression.

Sequences for Two Rescuers in CPR

Two rescuers should be able to coordinate and perform the following sequences, as appropriate. All techniques should be performed, when appropriate, as described in Chapter 4.

Beginning Two-Rescuer CPR

When CPR Is in Progress with One Lay Rescuer

If CPR is in progress with one lay rescuer, the logical time for entrance of the two-healthcare-provider rescue team is immediately after the initial rescuer has completed a cycle of 15 compressions and 2 breaths:

One rescuer moves to the head, opens the airway, and checks for a pulse, while the other member of the team locates the area for external chest compressions and finds the proper hand position. This should take 5 seconds.

If there is no pulse, the ventilator gives one breath and the compressor begins external chest compressions at the rate of 80–100 per minute, counting "one and, two and, three and, four and, five."

At the end of the 5th compression a pause should be allowed for a ventilation (1–1.5 sec/inflation). The compression:ventilation ratio for two rescuers is 5:1. The pause for the rescue breath may be shorter or may be interposed if the victim is intubated, as faster inspiratory flow rates are

possible without the problem of gastric distention, regurgitation, and aspiration. After the airway is protected by the placement of an esophageal obturator airway or endotracheal tube, ventilations may be given in an asynchronous mode at a rate of 12–15 per minute.

When No CPR Is in Progress

If no CPR is in progress and both rescuers arrive on the scene at the same time, both must determine what needs to be done and start immediately, without wasting time. One rescuer should ensure that the EMS system is activated. If this person leaves the area, the other person should institute one-rescuer CPR.

If both persons are available, one rescuer should go to the head of the victim and proceed as follows:

1. Determine unresponsiveness.
2. Position the victim.
3. Open the airway.
4. Check for breathing.
5. If breathing is absent, say "No breathing" and give two ventilations.
6. Check for pulse. If there is no pulse, say "No pulse."

The second rescuer should, simultaneously,

1. Find the location for external chest compressions
2. Assume the proper hand position
3. Initiate external chest compressions after the first rescuer states "No pulse." (See Figures 39 and 40.)

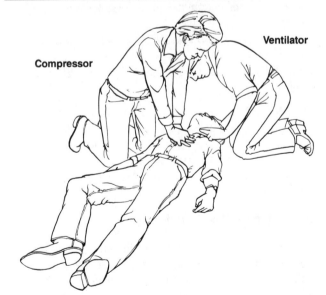

Figure 39. Two-rescuer CPR: No CPR in progress; two healthcare providers arrive simultaneously. The ventilator assesses the victim; the compressor assumes the proper position for external chest compressions.

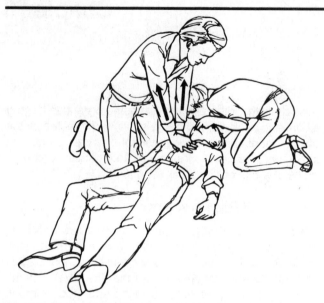

Figure 40. Two-rescuer CPR: Pause after the 5th external chest compression as ventilator gives a rescue breath.

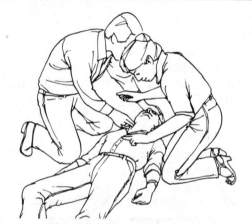

Figure 41. Two-rescuer CPR: Compressor and ventilator switch positions.

When CPR Is in Progress with One Healthcare Provider

If CPR is in progress with one healthcare provider, the entrance of a second healthcare-provider rescuer should be at the end of a cycle, after the check for a pulse by the first rescuer. The new cycle starts with one ventilation by the first rescuer, and the second rescuer becomes the compressor.

Monitoring the Victim

The victim's condition must be monitored to assess the effectiveness of the rescue effort. The ventilator assumes this responsibility for monitoring the pulse and breathing, which serves to

1. Evaluate the effectiveness of compressions
2. Determine if and when the victim resumes spontaneous circulation and breathing

To assess the effectiveness of the partner's external chest compressions, the pulse should be checked during the compressions. To determine if the victim has resumed spontaneous breathing and circulation, chest compressions must be stopped for 5 seconds at about the end of the first minute and every few minutes thereafter. When the compressor is fatigued, the rescuers should exchange places.

Switch Procedures

Switch on Opposite Sides

Two-rescuer CPR can be performed more smoothly and effectively when the rescuers are on opposite sides of the victim. This permits exchanging positions when necessary without interrupting the 5:1 sequence. The switch is initiated when the rescuer performing compressions directs that a switch take place at the end of a 5:1 sequence. The rescuer who is performing ventilations, after giving a breath, moves into position to give compressions and locates the proper hand position. The rescuer giving compressions, after the 5th compression, moves to the victim's head and checks the pulse for 5 seconds (Figure 41). If no pulse is felt, the rescuer at the victim's head gives a breath and tells the rescuer at the chest to "continue CPR." If there is a pulse but no breathing, the condition should be indicated and appropriate ventilation and monitoring continued. (See Figure 42 for a more detailed description of switching.)

Topics that relate to 1) switching procedures when both rescuers are on the same side of the victim, 2) two rescuers arriving at an emergency situation simultaneously, and 3) help from an untrained rescuer are not included in most basic rescuer courses. The following background information is provided for the instructor in answering questions or for inclusion in some BLS courses.

Switch from Same Side of Victim

In some cases, it may be necessary for both rescuers to perform CPR on the same side of the victim. CPR can still be performed effectively if the ventilator kneels beside the victim's head and the compressor kneels by the chest. Switching from the same side of the victim is not difficult, but it must be practiced and performed with precision or it will take too much time.

Compressor Initiates Switch: The compressor signals for a switch by changing the mnemonic while continuing chest compressions. The ventilator delivers a rescue breath after the 5th compression.

The Only Difference: After delivering the breath, the ventilator moves quickly behind and around the compressor and assumes the compressor position. The compressor moves to the victim's head to check the pulse and becomes the new ventilator.

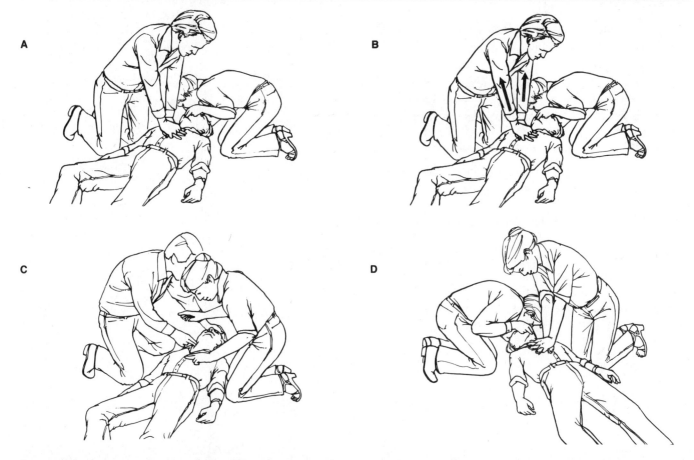

Figure 42. Procedure for switching responsibilities for compressions and ventilations. (A) Compressor changes mnemonic, indicating need for switch: "Change and, two and, three and, four and, five." (B) Ventilator delivers a full rescue breath at the completion of the 5th compression. (C) Ventilator moves to the victim's chest and finds the compression area after the compressor delivers the 5th compression. The compressor moves to the victim's head and completes a pulse and breathing check. (D) The new ventilator delivers a breath, signaling the beginning of a new cycle of 5 compressions and 1 ventilation.

Completed Switch: The new compressor finds the correct hand position and waits to begin compressions, positioned beside the victim's chest. The new ventilator immediately moves to the victim's head, completes the pulse and breathing check, and proceeds with appropriate maneuvers.

How an Untrained Rescuer Can Help

An untrained rescuer can help a trained rescuer who is performing one-rescuer CPR in three ways:

- By going for help
- By monitoring pulse and breathing, with some direction
- In some cases, by joining the first rescuer in CPR

As a rule, the untrained person should be sent for help. If help is already on the way, the novice may monitor the effectiveness of CPR. A brief explanation of how to assess the victim's carotid pulse and breathing may be given while continuing CPR without interruption.

Explain CPR

If the single rescuer is exhausted, it may be best to have the novice help perform CPR briefly so that the initial rescuer can regain his or her strength and resume CPR until help arrives. Since compressions are easier to learn by observation than is rescue breathing, tell the novice to watch what is being done and to copy the movements carefully. Tell the novice to watch how the chest is compressed.

- Point out the hand location on the victim's chest.
- Indicate that the fingers must be lifted off the chest, leaving only the heel of the hand in contact with the chest.
- Explain how to keep the arms perfectly straight and the shoulders over the victim's chest.

Novice Takes Over

The first rescuer should observe the novice's hands as the proper position is located.

- Alert the novice to be prepared to assume exactly the same chest position as the first rescuer's.
- Remind the novice that chest compressions must begin immediately and be continued without interruption.
- Explain the signal: "When I say 'Now!' push my hands out of the way, link your fingers, and start compressing."

As soon as the novice has begun compressions, the first rescuer should begin rescue breathing.

Monitor the Novice

While performing rescue breathing, the experienced rescuer must constantly monitor the novice's performance and make corrections in technique.

As soon as strength is regained, the experienced rescuer should resume one-person CPR unless the novice is performing absolutely adequate compressions.

Chapter 7

Foreign Body Airway Obstruction Management (First Aid for Choking)

Obstructed Airways — Causes and Precautions

Upper airway obstruction can cause unconsciousness and cardiopulmonary arrest, but far more often upper airway obstruction is caused by unconsciousness and cardiopulmonary arrest.

An unconscious patient can develop airway obstruction when the tongue falls backward into the pharynx, obstructing the upper airway. The epiglottis can block the entrance of the airway in an unconscious victim. Regurgitation of stomach contents into the pharynx, resulting in an obstructed airway, can occur during cardiopulmonary arrest or during resuscitative attempts. Head and facial injuries may also result in blood clots obstructing the upper airway, particularly if the patient is unconscious.

Obstruction of the airway by a foreign body (choking) usually occurs during eating. The National Safety Council[1] reported that foreign body obstruction of the airway accounted for approximately 3,100 deaths in 1984. Management of upper airway obstruction should be taught within the context of basic life support because, if the victim becomes unconscious, it is associated with ventilatory and circulatory problems. Any victim, especially from younger age groups, who suddenly stops breathing, becomes cyanotic, and falls unconscious for no apparent reason, should have foreign body airway obstruction considered in the differential diagnosis.

In adults, meat is the most common cause of foreign body airway obstruction, although a variety of other foods and foreign bodies have been the cause of choking in children and some adults. Common factors associated with choking on food include

1. Large, poorly chewed pieces of food
2. Elevated blood alcohol
3. Upper and/or lower dentures

This emergency, when it occurs in restaurants, has been mistaken for a heart attack, giving rise to the name "cafe coronary."[2]

The following precautions may prevent foreign body airway obstruction:

1. Cutting food into small pieces and chewing slowly and thoroughly, especially if wearing dentures
2. Avoiding laughing and talking during chewing and swallowing
3. Avoiding excessive intake of alcohol before and during meals
4. Preventing children from walking, running, or playing with food or foreign objects in their mouths
5. Keeping foreign objects, (e.g., marbles, beads, thumbtacks) away from infants and small children

Recognizing Foreign Body Airway Obstruction (Choking)

Because early recognition of airway obstruction is the key to successful management, it is important to distinguish this emergency from fainting, stroke, heart attack, epilepsy, drug overdose, or other conditions that cause sudden respiratory failure but that are managed differently.

Foreign bodies may cause either partial airway obstruction or complete airway obstruction. With partial airway obstruction, the victim may be capable of either "good air exchange" or "poor air exchange." With good air exchange, the victim can cough forcefully, although frequently there is wheezing between coughs. As long as good air exchange continues, the victim should be encouraged to persist with spontaneous coughing and breathing efforts. At this point, do not interfere with attempts to expel the foreign body; stay with the victim and monitor these attempts. If partial airway obstruction persists, activate the EMS system.

Poor air exchange may occur initially, or good air exchange may progress to poor air exchange, as indicated by a weak, ineffective cough, a high-pitched noise while inhaling, increased respiratory difficulty, and possibly, cyanosis. A partial obstruction with poor air exchange should be managed as if it were a complete airway obstruction.

With complete airway obstruction the victim is unable to speak, breathe, or cough and may clutch the neck between the thumb and fingers (Figure 43). (People

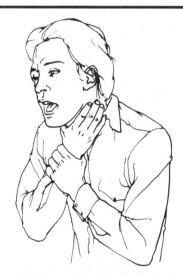

Figure 43. Universal distress signal for foreign body airway obstruction.

should be encouraged to use this sign, the universal distress signal.) Ask the victim if he/she is choking. Movement of air will be absent if complete airway obstruction is present. Oxygen saturation in the blood will decrease rapidly because the obstructed airway prevents entry of air into the lungs. The brain will develop an oxygen deficit resulting in unconsciousness, and death will follow rapidly if prompt action is not taken.

Management of Foreign Body Airway Obstruction

The Heimlich Maneuver

Subdiaphragmatic abdominal thrusts, popularly referred to as "the Heimlich maneuver," are recommended for relieving foreign body airway obstruction.[3] (The term "abdominal thrusts" has been used synonymously with "the Heimlich maneuver" since 1976.[4] For the sake of uniformity, "the Heimlich maneuver" should be used — but interchanged with the more descriptive "subdiaphragmatic abdominal thrusts" or "abdominal thrusts," depending on the circumstances.)

A subdiaphragmatic abdominal thrust, by elevating the diaphragm, can force air from the lungs in sufficient quantity to create an artificial cough intended to move and expel an obstructing foreign body in an airway.[5–11] Each individual thrust should be administered with the intent of relieving the obstruction. An important consideration during application of the maneuver is possible damage to internal organs (see "Complications," below).[12, 13] The rescuer's hands should never be placed on the xiphoid process of the sternum or on the lower margins of rib cage. They should be below this area but above the navel and in the midline. Regurgitation may occur as a result of abdominal thrusts. Training and proper performance should minimize these problems.

Conscious Victim — Standing or Sitting [3, 9, 10, 14]

The rescuer should stand behind the victim, wrap his or her arms around the victim's waist, and proceed as follows (Figure 44): Make a fist with one hand. Place the thumb side of the fist against the victim's abdomen, in the midline slightly above the navel and well below the tip of the xiphoid process. Grasp the fist with the other hand. Press the fist into the victim's abdomen with a quick upward thrust. Each new thrust should be a separate and distinct movement. The thrusts should be repeated until the foreign body is expelled or the victim becomes unconscious.

Unconscious Victim — Lying

The victim should be placed in the supine position with the face up (Figure 45). The rescuer should kneel astride the victim's thighs and place the heel of one hand against the victim's abdomen, in the midline slightly above the navel and well below the tip of the xiphoid, and the second hand directly on top of the first. The rescuer

should then press into the abdomen with a quick upward thrust. If the rescuer is in the correct position, he/she has a natural midabdominal position and is thus unlikely to direct the thrust to the right or left. A rescuer too short to reach around the waist of a victim who is conscious can use this technique. The rescuer can use his/her body weight to perform the maneuver. It may be necessary to repeat the thrust 6–10 times to clear the airway.

Figure 44. Subdiaphragmatic abdominal thrust (the Heimlich maneuver) administered to a conscious (standing) victim of foreign body airway obstruction.

Figure 45. Subdiaphragmatic abdominal thrust (the Heimlich maneuver) administered to an unconscious (lying) victim of foreign body airway obstruction — astride position.

Self-Administered Abdominal Thrusts

Treatment of one's own complete foreign body airway obstruction is as follows: Make a fist with one hand, place the thumb side on the abdomen above the navel and below the xiphoid process, grasp the fist with the other hand, and then press inward and upward toward the diaphragm with a quick motion. If this is unsuccessful, press the upper abdomen quickly over any firm surface such as the back of a chair, side of a table, or porch railing. Several thrusts may be needed to clear the airway.

Complications

A significant consideration in either abdominal or chest thrusts (see "Chest Thrusts for Special Cases" in this chapter) is possible internal damage, such as rupture or laceration of abdominal or thoracic organs. The rescuer's hands should never be placed on the xiphoid process of the sternum or on the lower margins of the rib cage. In older persons the use of abdominal thrusts has less risk than chest thrusts for the fracture of brittle ribs. Regurgitation can occur after an abdominal thrust. Training and proper performance will minimize these problems.

Manual Removal of Foreign Bodies

If a foreign body can be seen in the mouth, it should be removed with the fingers. If a foreign body is strongly suspected but cannot be seen, abdominal thrusts may result in moving or dislodging it so that it is more accessible for removal.

Finger Sweep

1. The finger sweep (Figure 46) is performed only on the unconscious victim.
2. With the head up, the rescuer opens the victim's mouth by grasping both the tongue and the lower jaw between his/her thumb and fingers and lifting (tongue–jaw lift). This action draws the tongue from the back of the throat and away from the foreign body. The obstruction may be partially relieved by this maneuver. If the rescuer is unable to open the mouth with tongue–jaw lift, the crossed-finger technique may be used (Figure 47). The rescuer opens the mouth by crossing the index finger and thumb and pushing the teeth apart.
3. The index finger of the rescuer's available hand is inserted along the inside of the cheek and deeply into the throat to the base of the tongue. A hooking motion is used to dislodge the foreign body and maneuver it into the mouth for removal. Occasionally, it is necessary to use the index finger to push the foreign body against the opposite side of the throat to dislodge and lift it. Take care not to force the object deeper into the airway. If the foreign body comes within reach, grasp and remove it.

Figure 46. Finger sweep maneuver administered to an unconscious victim of foreign body airway obstruction.

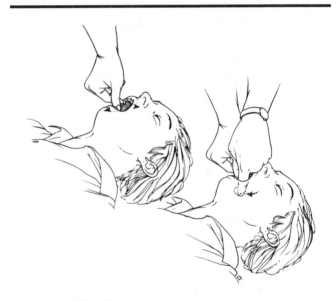

Figure 47. Crossed-finger technique for opening the airway.

Devices for Removing Foreign Bodies

Instructions for the use of special devices should *not* be part of a BLS course for the general public. The Instructor should mention devices only if questioned and then only to condemn their use by laypersons. *The use of the following devices is restricted to properly trained and authorized medical and paramedical personnel.* The Kelly Clamp and Magill Forceps are two devices designed to relieve airway obstruction by grasping the foreign body. These devices should be used only with direct visualization of the foreign body by either a laryngoscope or a tongue blade and flashlight.

Chest Thrusts for Special Cases

Chest thrusts (Figure 48) may be used only in the advanced stages of pregnancy or in the markedly obese victim when the rescuer cannot apply abdominal thrusts effectively.

Conscious Victim — Sitting or Standing

The rescuer should stand behind the victim, rescuer's arms directly under victim's armpits, and encircle the victim's chest. The rescuer should place the thumb side of his or her fist on the middle of the breastbone, taking care to avoid the xiphoid process and the margins of the rib cage. The rescuer should then grab his or her fist with the other hand and perform backward thrusts until the foreign body is expelled or the victim becomes unconscious. Each thrust should be administered with the intent of relieving the obstruction.

Unconscious Victim — Lying

The rescuer places the victim on his/her back and kneels close to the side of his/her body (Figure 49). The hand position for the application of chest thrusts is the same as that for external heart compressions, e.g., in the adult, the heel of the hand is on the lower half of the sternum. Each thrust should be delivered slowly, distinctly, and with the intent of relieving the obstruction.

Recommended Sequences

The Conscious Victim and the Victim Who Becomes Unconscious

a. Identify airway obstruction: Ask the victim if he or she is choking.
b. Apply the Heimlich maneuver (subdiaphragmatic abdominal thrusts) until the foreign body is expelled or the victim becomes unconscious.
c. Open the mouth of the now unconscious victim and perform the finger sweep.
d. Open the airway and attempt rescue breathing.
e. If unable to ventilate, perform additional (6–10) subdiaphragmatic abdominal thrusts.
f. Open the mouth and perform a finger sweep.
g. Attempt to ventilate.
h. Repeat the sequence of Heimlich maneuver, finger sweep, and attempt to ventilate.
i. Persist in these efforts as long as necessary.
j. A second person, if available, should activate the EMS as soon as possible.

The Unconscious Victim

If a rescuer has found an unconscious victim and is unable to ventilate, he/she should reposition the head and try again to ventilate. If unsuccessful, subdiaphragmatic abdominal thrusts (the Heimlich maneuver), followed by the finger sweep, should be performed. If unsuccessful in removing the foreign body, repeat the sequence of thrusts, finger sweep, and attempt to ventilate.

Figure 48. Chest thrust administered to an conscious victim (standing) of foreign body airway obstruction.

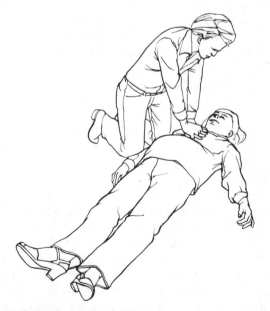

Figure 49. Chest thrust administered to an unconscious victim (lying) of foreign body airway obstruction.

Summary

1. The Heimlich maneuver (subdiaphragmatic abdominal thrusts) is the recommended technique for foreign body airway obstruction removal in the adult. The use of only this method, which is more effective than and as safe as any other single method, will simplify training programs and should result in better skills retention.

2. It is recommended that chest thrusts be used in the markedly obese person and in the advanced stages of pregnancy when there is no room between the enlarging uterus and the rib cage in which to perform the thrusts.[10, 15] These incidents are rare.

3. Under no circumstances should students practice subdiaphragmatic abdominal thrusts (the Heimlich maneuver) on each other during CPR training.

4. The use of devices by persons who are not proficient in their use is unacceptable and is seen as a distinct threat to the well-being of patients in need of emergency airway care.

References

1. *Accident Facts*, 1984 ed. Chicago, National Safety Council, 1984, p 7.
2. Haugen RK: The cafe coronary. *JAMA* 1963;186:142–143.
3. Heimlich HJ: A life-saving maneuver to prevent food-choking. *JAMA* 1975;234:398–401.
4. Report on Emergency Airway Management, Committee on Emergency Medical Services, Assembly of Life Sciences, National Research Council, National Academy of Sciences, Washington, DC, 1976.
5. Day RL, Crelin ES, DuBois AB: Choking: The Heimlich abdominal thrust vs. back blows: An approach to measurement of inertial and aerodynamic forces. *Pediatrics* 1982;70:113–119.
6. Day RL, DuBois AB: Treatment of choking. *Pediatrics* 1983;71:300–301.
7. Day RL: Differing opinions on the emergency treatment of choking. *Pediatrics* 1983;71:976–977.
8. Patrick EA: *Decision Analysis in Medicine Methods and Applications*. Boca Raton, CRC Press Inc, 1979, pp 90–93.
9. Heimlich HJ, Hoffman KA, Canestri FR: Food-choking and drowning deaths prevented by external subdiaphragmatic compression: Physiological basis. *Ann Thorac Surg* 1975;20:188–195.
10. Heimlich HJ, Uhtley MH: The Heimlich maneuver. *Clin Symp Ciba* 1979;31(3):22.
11. Patrick EA: Choking: A questionnaire to find the most effective treatment. *Emergency* 1980;12:59–63.
12. Visintine RE, Baick CH: Ruptured stomach after Heimlich maneuver. *JAMA* 1975;234:415.
13. Palmer E: The Heimlich maneuver misused. *Current Prescribing* 1979;5:45–49.
14. Heimlich HJ: Pop goes the cafe coronary. *Emergency Med* 1974;6:154–155.
15. Standards and Guidelines for Cardiopulmonary Resuscitation (CPR) and Emergency Cardiac Care (ECC). *JAMA* 1980;244(5):461.

Pediatric Basic Life Support

Chapter 8

Cardiopulmonary resuscitation in the pediatric age group should be part of a community-wide effort that smoothly integrates pediatric basic life support, pediatric advanced life support, and pediatric postresuscitation care. Except in the newborn period, the number of children who require resuscitation is small; for best results, therefore, each community must ensure that its emergency medical services personnel are optimally trained and equipped to care for pediatric emergencies. There is evidence that this is not currently the case.[1]

Pediatric CPR and foreign body airway obstruction management are treated as addenda to many basic life support courses. The reasons for this are diverse but include the unavailability of a good child manikin, lack of learner interest, and the discomfort of instructors with the material. The basic life support (BLS) course, though, is a perfect opportunity for teaching the skills of resuscitating infants and children and for emphasizing methods of prevention (which to some extent will eliminate the necessity for CPR).

Additional information is available on this subject in the student manual *Textbook of Pediatric Basic Life Support,* which emphasizes prevention.

Basic Principles of BLS in Infants and Children

Causes of Cardiopulmonary Arrest

Cardiac arrest in the pediatric age group is rarely primarily of cardiac origin; more commonly, it results from a low oxygen level secondary to respiratory difficulty or arrest. Since the cardiac arrest is the result of a long period of hypoxemia, it is not surprising that outcomes of cardiopulmonary resuscitation (CPR) in children who have suffered a cardiac arrest have been poor.[2, 3] On the other hand, the outcome of resuscitation from respiratory arrest, before the development of cardiac arrest, is considerably better.[2] It should be possible to improve the current poor results with an educational program — directed at parents, child care personnel, and members of the emergency medical services (EMS) system — that emphasizes prevention, early recognition of the child in distress, and rapid intervention before cardiac arrest occurs.

The major events that may necessitate resuscitation include:

1. Injuries
2. Suffocation caused by foreign bodies (i.e., toys, foods, plastic covers, etc.)
3. Smoke inhalation
4. Sudden infant death syndrome
5. Infections, especially of the respiratory tract

Injuries account for nearly 9,000 pediatric fatalities annually in the United States and represent approximately 44% of deaths in children between the ages of 1 and 14 years. Of these, 45% involve motor vehicles, 17% drowning, and 21% burns, firearms, and poisoning. In children under one year of age, 41% of accidental deaths involve poisons, suffocation, or motor vehicles.[4] Death rates and causes among infants and children are tabulated in Table 2.

Table 2. Deaths and Death Rates from Accidents, Suicide, and Homicide for Infants and Children in Three Age Groups, 1985

	< 1 yr.		1–4 yr.		5–14 yr.	
	Deaths	Rate*	Deaths	Rate*	Deaths	Rate*
All causes	40,030	1067.8	7,339	51.4	8,933	26.3
All accidents	890	23.7	2,856	20.0	4,252	12.5
Motor vehicle	179	4.8	1,016	7.1	2,319	6.8
Fires and flames	111	3.0	613	4.3	453	1.3
Drowning and submersion	88	2.3	587	4.1	532	1.6
Falls	45	1.2	80	0.6	71	0.2
Firearms	2	0.1	41	0.3	235	0.7
Inhalation and ingestion of food or object	170	4.5	102	0.7	51	0.2
Mechanical suffocation	171	4.6	71	0.5	93	0.3
Poisoning, accidental	18	0.5	62	0.4	52	0.2
Other	106	2.8	284	2.0	446	1.3
Suicide	—	—	—	—	278	0.8
Homicide	200	5.3	348	2.4	417	1.2

* Rates per 100,000 population in specified age groups. Adapted from data from the National Center for Health Statistics.[5]

Motor Vehicle Accidents

By far the largest number of deaths and serious injuries in children involve the automobile[6] and are the result of inadequate restraints. Despite the fact that those who use seat belts have 60% less chance of serious injury and 35% less chance of death than those who do not use them, fewer than 20% of drivers presently use seat belts. In the 1- to 10-year age group, more than 90% are riding in cars without restraints, and even in situations where parents are using seat belts, it has been found that 75% of children are not similarly protected. The General Motors Corporation has warned that in a 30 mph collision, a 10-pound child can exert a 300-pound force against the parent's grip, making it almost impossible to hold the child safely even if the parent is wearing a seat belt.[7] More than half the states have mandated the use of some form of restraint for children, and many have specified the use of a protective car seat with harness for infants. Infant seats can be rented from car-rental agencies and are available on loan from many healthcare institutions providing services to children.

Airway Obstruction

Airway obstruction leading to asphyxia is a leading cause of death and disability in children. It can be caused by a foreign body, such as a toy or peanut, or may be caused by an infection that causes swelling of the airway, such as occurs in croup or epiglottitis. The differentiation between a foreign body and an infectious cause is important since in the latter case, going through the steps of dislodging a foreign body will not be helpful, can be dangerous, and will cause delay in transporting the child to an appropriate advanced life support facility. The symptoms of croup or epiglottitis may be those of airway obstruction, and the underlying cause can be suspected at the time of an emergency by the circumstances of the event. A child who has been ill with fever and has a barking cough and progressive airway obstruction needs transportation to the nearest emergency facility. The child, previously healthy, who chokes while eating and has difficulty in breathing may need relief of foreign body airway obstruction.

Poisoning

Poisoning through accidental ingestion is most common in the 1- to 4-year age group and usually involves medication (including aspirin), kerosene, lighter fluid, cleaning agents, and caustic substances such as lye. Most accidents occur in the home and result from a combination of easy accessibility and childhood curiosity.

Sudden Infant Death Syndrome

The sudden infant death syndrome (SIDS) is the single largest cause of death in infants between the ages of 1 month and 1 year and accounts for 8,000–10,000 deaths annually. The death is, as the name implies, sudden and unexpected. It is rare in the first few weeks of life and reaches a peak incidence at 2–3 months, again becoming less frequent toward the latter part of the first year and rare after 12 months. Some high-risk factors have been identified, but the cause of death remains unknown. Occasionally, an otherwise healthy infant is found not breathing and is successfully resuscitated with CPR. Such a survivor is termed a *near miss* or *aborted* SIDS. Many of these infants are sent home with respiratory and heart rate monitors, and the parents are instructed in infant CPR.

Prevention

The vast majority of emergency situations requiring CPR and airway obstruction management are preventable; therefore, special attention must be given to providing environments for children that are safe and protective without suppressing their need for exploration and discovery. Children should be taught respect for matches and fires, and young children should not be left unsupervised. Toys given to toddlers should be carefully examined for small parts that could be aspirated. Beads, small toys, marbles, peanuts, and such must be kept away from infants and preschool children. In automobiles, age-appropriate restraints, including infant car seats and seatbelts, should be used. Children should be taught to swim, and water safety should be emphasized. It is important to remember that time spent mastering CPR is much less productive than time spent preventing the situation leading to its need.

Differences in Infant, Child, and Adult BLS

The basic steps, or actions, of CPR (with foreign body airway obstruction management) are the same whether the victim is an infant, a child, or an adult. They include:

- Assessment: determining unresponsiveness or respiratory difficulty
- Calling for help
- Positioning the victim
- Opening the airway
- Assessment: determining breathlessness
- If necessary, recognizing and managing an obstructed airway
- Performing rescue breathing
- Assessment: determining pulselessness
- Activating the EMS system
- Performing external chest compressions

Differences in BLS among infants, children, and adults relate to the cause of the emergency, the stage of physical development of the victim, and variations in sizes of victims. These factors dictate some of the priorities in BLS, so there are differences between infants and small children and between small children and older children/ adults. (Older, more mature children, i.e., over 8 years of age, are treated as adults for the purposes of BLS.) Variations in CPR techniques for infants, children, and adults are summarized in Table 3; variations in foreign body airway obstruction management techniques are explained in a later section in this chapter.

Size of Victim: There is considerable variation in children's sizes, even at the same ages. For the purpose of BLS, an infant is defined as anyone younger than 1 year and a child is anyone between 1 and 8 years of age. It is recognized that some large infants (younger than 1 year) might be mistaken for a child (1 to 8 years) and that a small adolescent might be mistaken for a child. These definitions are guidelines only. In an emergency a slight error one way or the other is not critical.

The Sequence of CPR

AIRWAY
Assessment: Determine Unresponsiveness or Respiratory Difficulty

The rescuer must quickly assess the extent of any injury and determine whether the child is unconscious. Special care must be taken if the victim has sustained head or neck trauma so as not to cause spinal cord injury. Unconsciousness is determined by gently shaking the victim to elicit a response. If the child is struggling to breathe but is conscious, the child should be transported as rapidly as possible to an advanced life support facility. Children will often find the best position in which to keep a partially obstructed airway open and should therefore be allowed to maintain the position affording them the greatest comfort.

Call for Help

After determining unresponsiveness or respiratory difficulty, the rescuer should call out for help. If the rescuer is alone and the child obviously is not breathing, CPR should be performed for 1 minute before calling for help.

Table 3. Variations in CPR Techniques for the Infant, Child, and Adult

Age	Infant 0–1 yr.	Child 1–8 yr.	Adult <8 yr.
Shake and shout	Shake only	Yes	Yes
Call for help	Yes	Yes	Yes
Position victim	Yes	Yes	Yes
Open airway	Yes	Yes	Yes
Look, listen, feel for breath	Yes	Yes	Yes
Two breaths	Yes	Yes	Yes
Check pulse	Brachial	Carotid	Carotid
Activate EMS	Yes	Yes	Yes
Locate hand position	Lower sternum	Lower sternum	Lower sternum
Compress with	2–3 fingers	Heel of one hand	Heel of two hands
Compression depth	½–1 inch	1–1½ inches	1½–2 inches
Compressions per minute	At least 100	80–100	80–100
Compression:ventilation ratio	5:1	5:1	15:2 or 5:1*

* Rates for one-rescuer (15:2) and two-rescuer (5:1) adult CPR.

Position the Victim

In order for CPR to be effective, the victim must be lying on his/her back on a firm, flat surface. Great care must be taken in moving a child into this position, especially if there is evidence of head and neck injury. The circumstances in which the child is found should influence the care that may be needed in positioning him or her. The likelihood of neck, spine, or bone injuries is greater if a child is found unconscious at the scene of an accident — for example, at the base of a tree — than if an infant is found in bed not breathing. The size of the child will also influence how he/she is positioned, but the principle to bear in mind is that the child must be turned as a unit, with firm support of the head and neck so that the head does not roll, twist, or tilt backward or forward.

Open the Airway

The smaller air passages of an infant or child can easily be obstructed by mucus, blood, vomitus, or, in an unconscious victim, the tongue. The tongue is attached to the lower jaw; with loss of consciousness the muscles relax and the tongue falls back, obstructing the airway.[8] The first maneuver, after determining unconsciousness and maneuvering the victim into the supine position, is to open the airway. This is accomplished by head-tilt/chin-lift.[8, 9] If the child is having respiratory difficulty but is conscious, time should not be wasted on an attempt to open the airway; the child should be transported to an ALS facility as rapidly as possible.

Head-Tilt/Chin-Lift

The rescuer places the hand closest to the child's head on the forehead and tilts the head gently back, in infants, into a sniffing or neutral position or, in children, slightly further back (Figure 50). Some believe that overextension of the head closes the trachea in small babies; there is no data that this is so, but since it is unnecessary, overextension is best avoided. The head should not be tilted in suspected neck injury; jaw-thrust, without head-tilt, may be used instead.

To augment head-tilt, the rescuer lifts the chin, with its attached structures, including the tongue, from the airway. The fingers, but not the thumb, of the hand away from the victim's head are placed under the bony part of the lower jaw at the chin, and the chin is lifted upward. So as not to obstruct the airway, care must be exercised not to close the mouth completely or to push on the soft parts of the under-chin. Except in cases of suspected neck injury, the rescuer's other hand continues to tilt the head backward.

Jaw-Thrust

The rescuer places two or three fingers under each side of the lower jaw at its angle and lifts the jaw upward (Figure 51). The rescuer's elbows should rest on the sur-

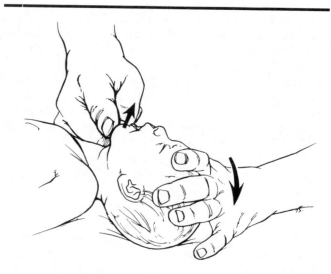

Figure 50. Head-tilt/chin-lift.

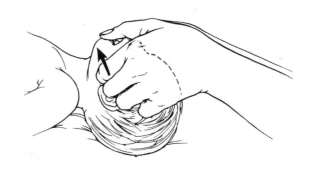

Figure 51. Jaw-thrust.

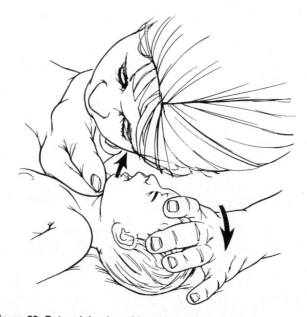

Figure 52. Determining breathlessness while maintaining head-tilt/chin-lift.

face on which the victim is lying. Jaw-thrust may be accompanied by slight head-tilt or can be used alone. Jaw-thrust, without head-tilt, is the safest technique for opening the airway when neck injury is suspected.

BREATHING
Assessment: Determine Whether the Victim Is Breathing

If it is unclear whether the victim is breathing, the airway is opened and, while patency is being maintained, the rescuer places his or her ear close to the victim's mouth and nose (Figure 52) while

LOOKing at the chest and abdomen for movement
LISTENing for exhaled air and
FEELing for exhaled air flow

If the child is breathing, continued patency of the airway must be maintained. If no breathing is detected, the rescuer must breathe for the victim.

Breathe for the Victim

If after the airway is opened the victim does not breathe, rescue breathing must be applied in order to provide the victim's lungs with oxygen. While continuing to maintain patency of the airway, the rescuer takes a breath and makes a seal between his/her mouth and the mouth, or mouth and nose, of the victim. If the victim is an infant, the rescuer's mouth will make a tight seal with the mouth and nose (Figure 53). If the victim is larger, the nose is pinched tightly with the fingers of the hand that is maintaining head-tilt, and a mouth-to-mouth seal is made (Figure 54). Two breaths (1–1.5 sec/inflation) are given, with a pause between for the rescuer to take a breath.

The volume of air in an infant's lungs is smaller than that in an adult's, and an infant's air passages also are considerably smaller, with resistance to flow potentially quite high. Since these differences are relative, it is impossible to make a recommendation about the force or volume of the rescue breaths. There are three critical things to remember in this regard:

1. Rescue breaths are the single most important maneuver in assisting a nonbreathing child victim.
2. An appropriate volume is that volume which will make the chest rise and fall.
3. By giving the breaths slowly (1–1.5 sec/inflation), an adequate volume will be provided at the lowest possible pressure, thereby avoiding gastric distention.[9, 10]

If air enters freely and the chest rises, the airway is clear. If air does not enter freely (i.e., the chest does not rise) the airway is obstructed. Improper opening of the airway is the most common cause of obstruction, and head-tilt/chin-lift should be adjusted. If a repeated rescue breathing attempt does not allow air to enter freely as evidenced by lack of chest movement, a foreign body obstruction should be suspected (see "Foreign Body Airway Obstruction Management" in this chapter).

Gastric Distention: Rescue breathing, especially if rapidly applied, can cause gastric distention,[9, 10] which, if excessive, can interfere with rescue breathing by elevating the diaphragm, thus decreasing lung volume. The incidence of gastric distention can be minimized by limiting the rate of chest inflation and the ventilation volume to the point at which the chest rises, thereby not exceeding the esophageal opening pressure. Attempts at relieving gastric distention by pressure on the abdomen should be avoided because of the danger of aspiration of stomach contents into the lungs.

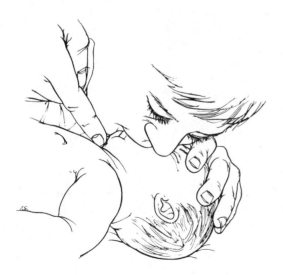

Figure 53. Rescue breathing with an airtight seal around the mouth and nose.

Figure 54. Mouth-to-mouth seal.

Gastric decompression should be attempted only if the abdomen is so tense that ventilation is ineffective. In such a situation the victim's entire body is turned as a unit onto the side, with the head down if possible, before pressure is applied to the abdomen.

CIRCULATION
Assessment: Determine Whether There Is a Pulse

Ineffective or absent cardiac contractions are recognized by the absence of a pulse in a large central artery. In a child over 1 year of age the carotid is the most central and accessible artery; under 1 year of age, the short, chubby neck of the infant makes the carotid difficult to palpate, so the brachial artery is recommended instead.[11] The femoral pulse is often used by healthcare providers in a hospital setting; however, it is recommended that lay rescuers be instructed in locating the carotid and brachial arteries only.

The carotid artery lies on the side of the neck between the windpipe and the strap muscles. While maintaining head-tilt with one hand on the forehead, the rescuer locates the victim's Adam's apple with two or three fingers of the other hand. The fingers are then slid into the groove, on the side closest to the rescuer, between the trachea and the neck muscles; and the artery is gently palpated (Figure 55).

The brachial pulse is located on the inside of the upper arm, between elbow and shoulder. With the rescuer's thumb on the outside of the arm, the index and middle fingers are pressed gently until the pulse is felt (Figure 56).

If There Is a Pulse

When there is a pulse but no breathing, rescue breathing should be initiated and continued until spontaneous breathing resumes. For an infant the rescue breathing rate should be once every 3 seconds, or 20 times a minute; for a child once every 4 seconds, or 15 times a minute.

If There Is No Pulse

If a pulse is not present, a diagnosis of cardiac arrest is made and chest compressions must be initiated and coordinated with rescue breathing.

Activate the EMS System

If a second rescuer is present or arrives to help, one rescuer should activate the EMS system by calling the local emergency telephone number — in many communities, 911. (The emergency number should be widely publicized.) If no help is forthcoming, the decision when to leave the victim in order to telephone is a difficult one and is affected by a number of variables, including the probability of someone else arriving on the scene. If the res-

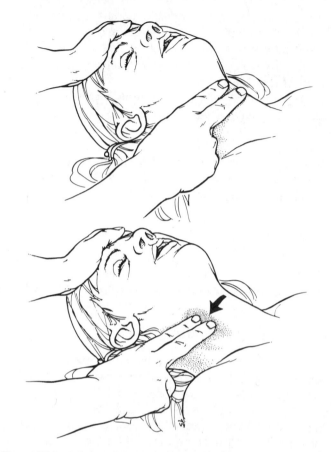

Figure 55. Locating and palpating the carotid artery pulse.

Figure 56. Locating and palpating the brachial pulse.

cuer is unable to activate the EMS system, the only option is to continue CPR.

The rescuer calling the EMS system should give the following information:

1. The location of the emergency — address, names of streets or landmarks
2. The phone number from which the call is being made
3. What happened — auto accident, drowning, etc.
4. The number of victims
5. The condition of the victim(s)
6. The nature of the aid being given
7. Any other information requested. To ensure this last item, *the caller should hang up last*

Perform Chest Compressions

The external chest compression technique consists of serial, rhythmic compressions of the chest by which blood is circulated to the vital organs (heart, lungs, and brain) to keep them viable until ALS care can be given. Chest compressions must always be accompanied by rescue breathing. The mechanism by which blood is circulated by chest compressions is still a subject of controversy. It is not clear whether this takes place by a change in the thoracic pressures, by direct compression of the heart, or by a combination of both[12-15]; but direct heart compression may be the more important mechanism in the pediatric age group.[16]

For optimal compressions the child must be in a horizontal supine position on a hard surface. In an infant, the hard surface can be the palm of the hand not performing the compressions; head-tilt is then provided by the weight of the head and a slight lift of the shoulders.

Recent evidence[17] has shown that the heart of the infant is lower in relation to the external chest landmarks than was previously thought. In the following recommendations, therefore, the area of compression is lower for infants than in previous standards.

In the Infant (Figure 57)

a. An imaginary line between the nipples is located over the breastbone.
b. The index finger of the hand furthest from the infant's head is placed just under the intermammary line where it intersects the sternum. The area of compression is one finger's width below this intersection. Because of wide variations in the relative sizes of rescuers' hands and infants' chests, these instructions are only guidelines; after finding the position for compressions, make sure that you are not on the xyphoid process.
c. Using the middle and ring fingers, the breastbone is compressed to a depth of ½–1 in. (1.3–2.5 cm) at a rate of at least 100 times/min.

d. At the end of each compression, pressure is released and the sternum is allowed to come to its normal position, without removing the fingers from the sternum. A smooth (without jerky movements) compression–relaxation rhythm should be developed in which equal time is allotted to each.

In the Child (Figure 58)

a. The lower margin of the victim's rib cage is located on the side next to the rescuer, with the middle and index fingers — while the hand nearest the victim's head maintains head tilt.
b. The margin of the rib cage is followed with the middle finger to the notch where the ribs and breastbone meet.
c. With the middle finger on this notch, the index finger is placed next to the middle finger.

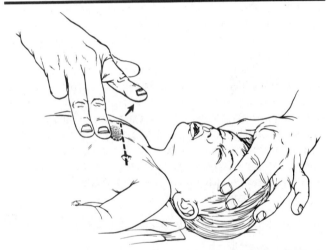

Figure 57. Locating finger position for chest compressions in an infant.

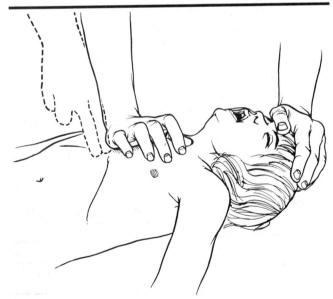

Figure 58. Locating hand position for chest compressions in a child.

d. While looking at the position of the index finger, lift that hand and place the heel of that hand next to where the index finger was, with the long axis of the heel parallel to that of the sternum.

e. The chest is compressed with one hand to a depth of 1–1½ in. (2.5–3.8 cm) at a rate of 80–100 times/min. The fingers should be kept off the ribs.

f. The compressions should be smooth, not jerky; the chest should be allowed to return to its resting position after each compression, but the hand should not be lifted off the chest. Each compression and relaxation phase should be equal in time.

g. If the child is large or above the age of approximately 8 years, the method described for adults in Chapter 4 should be used.

Coordinate Compressions and Rescue Breathing

External chest compressions must always be accompanied by rescue breathing. At the end of every fifth compression, a pause should be allowed for a ventilation (1–1.5 sec/inflation). In the infant and child the 5:1 compression/ventilation ratio is maintained for both one and two rescuers. The two-rescuer technique should be used only by healthcare providers. Since compressions must be briefly interrupted to allow for an adequate ventilation, compression rates of at least 100 per minute for infants and 80–100 per minute for children are recommended. The infant and child should be reassessed after 10 cycles of compressions and ventilations (approximately 1 minute) and every few minutes thereafter.

Foreign Body Airway Obstruction Management

More than 90% of deaths from foreign body aspiration in the pediatric age group occur in children less than 5 years old, and 65% are in infants. The 1985 National Conference noted the marked decline in pediatric deaths from foreign body aspiration since the last conference. The reason for this decline is not clear. Aspirated materials include foods (e.g., hot dogs, round candies, nuts, grapes)[18] and other small objects. Foreign body airway obstruction should be suspected in infants and children experiencing acute respiratory distress associated with coughing, gagging, or stridor (a high-pitched, noisy breathing).

Signs and symptoms of airway obstruction may also be due to infections that cause airway swelling, such as epiglottitis and croup. Children with an infectious cause of airway obstruction (e.g., a recent history of fever) need prompt attention in an ALS facility, and time should not be wasted in a futile attempt to relieve their obstruction. Attempts at clearing the airway should be considered for

1. Children whose aspiration is witnessed or strongly suspected
2. Unconscious, nonbreathing children whose airways remain obstructed despite the usual maneuvers to open it

In a witnessed or strongly suspected aspiration, the rescuer should encourage the child to persist with spontaneous coughing and breathing efforts as long as the cough is forceful. Relief of the obstruction should be attempted only if the cough is, or becomes, ineffective and/or there is increased respiratory difficulty accompanied by a high-pitched noise while inhaling (stridor). The EMS system should be activated as soon as a second rescuer is available.

The optimal method for relief of foreign body obstruction remains a matter of controversy, and further data is needed to distinguish opinions and personal experiences from objective facts. If the victim is a child, the Heimlich maneuver, which is a series of subdiaphragmatic abdominal thrusts, is recommended.[19-22] This maneuver, by increasing intrathoracic pressures, creates an artificial cough that forces air and, hopefully, a foreign body out of the airway. However, there is concern for potential intra-abdominal injury resulting from subdiaphragmatic abdominal thrusts in infants less than 1 year of age. In this age group, therefore, a combination of back blows and chest thrusts is to be recommended.[23] Some believe that in the infant this combination is an indirect application of the Heimlich maneuver.

Following maneuvers to remove an airway obstruction, the airway is opened using head-tilt/chin-lift, and if spontaneous breathing is absent, rescue breathing is performed. If the chest does not rise, the head is repositioned, the airway is opened, and rescue breathing is attempted again. If rescue breathing is still unsuccessful (the chest does not rise), maneuvers to relieve foreign body obstruction should be repeated.

Infant — Back Blows and Chest Thrusts

The infant is straddled over the rescuer's arm, with the head lower than the trunk; and the head is supported by firmly holding the jaw. The rescuer rests his/her forearm on his/her thigh and delivers four back blows forcefully with the heel of the hand between the infant's shoulder blades (Figure 59). After delivering the back blows, the rescuer places his free hand on the infant's back so that the victim is sandwiched between the two hands, one supporting the neck, jaw, and chest, while the other supports the back. While continuing to support the head and neck, the infant is turned, placed on the thigh with the head lower than the trunk, and four chest thrusts (Figure 60) are performed in the same location as external chest compressions (Figure 57) but at a slower rate. Rescuers whose hands are small may find it physically difficult to perform the back blows and chest thrusts in the described manner, especially if the infant is large. An alternate method is to lay the infant face down on the rescuer's lap, the head lower than the trunk, with the head firmly supported. After the four back blows have been performed, the infant is turned as a unit to the supine position and the chest thrusts performed.

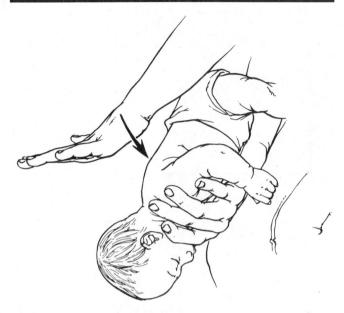

Figure 59. Back blow in an infant.

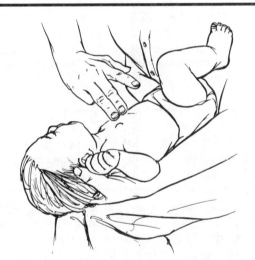

Figure 60. Chest thrust in an infant.

Child — Heimlich Maneuver (Abdominal Thrusts)

Conscious Victim — Standing or Sitting

The rescuer stands behind the victim and wraps his/her arms around the victim's waist, with one hand made into a fist (Figure 61). The thumb side of the fist should rest against the victim's abdomen in the midline slightly above the navel and well below the tip of the xiphoid process. The fist is grasped by the other hand and pressed into the victim's abdomen with a quick upward thrust. The rescuer's hands should not touch the xiphoid process or the lower margins of the rib cage because of possible damage to internal organs.[24, 25] Each thrust should be a separate and distinct movement.

Figure 61. Heimlich maneuver — conscious child, standing.

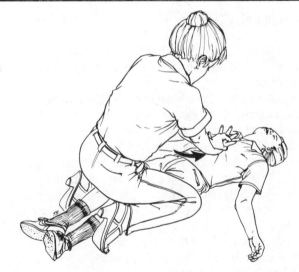

Figure 62. Heimlich maneuver — conscious or unconscious child, lying.

Conscious or Unconscious Victim — Lying

The rescuer positions the child face up on his or her back and kneels at the child's feet, if on the floor, or stands at the child's feet, if on a table[22] (Figure 62). (The astride position is not recommended for small children but may be used in the case of a large child.) The rescuer places the heel of one hand on the child's abdomen in the midline slightly above the navel and well below the rib cage. The other hand is placed on top of the first and pressed into the abdomen with a quick upward thrust. Care should be exercised to direct the thrusts upward in the midline and not to either side of the abdomen. Several thrusts may be necessary to expel the object. In small children the maneuver must be applied gently.

Manual Removal of Foreign Bodies

Blind finger sweeps are to be avoided in infants and children since the foreign body may be pushed back into the airway, causing further obstruction. In the unconscious, nonbreathing victim following the chest thrusts or subdiaphragmatic abdominal thrusts, the victim's mouth is opened by grasping both the tongue and the lower jaw between the thumb and finger and lifting (tongue–jaw lift). This action draws the tongue away from the back of the throat and may itself partially relieve the obstruction. If the foreign body is visualized, it should be removed.

Child Two-Rescuer CPR

The two-rescuer sequences described in Chapter 6 for adult victims can be used with child victims as well. There is no recommended two-rescuer sequence for infants, however, because no particular advantage is gained by using two rescuers and because involving two persons in performing infant CPR can be awkward.

Neonatal CPR

The specifications for ventilations and other chest compressions in the neonate or very small infant are summarized below.

An assisted ventilatory rate of 40–60 breaths/min should provide adequate ventilation.

There are two techniques for performing chest compressions in the neonate and small infant. One employs both thumbs placed on the lower third of the sternum, with the fingers encircling the torso and supporting the back (Figure 63). The thumbs should be positioned side-by-side on the sternum just below a line between the two nipples. In the very small infant the thumbs may have to be superimposed. Because of the potential for damaging the abdominal organs, the xiphoid portion of the sternum should not be compressed.

If the infant is large or the resuscitator's hands are too small to encircle the chest, two- or three-finger compressions to a depth of ½″ to ¾″ on the sternum one finger's breadth below the nipple line, but not over the xiphoid, are applied (see Chapter 8, Figure 57). The sternum is compressed at a rate of 120 times/min. The compression

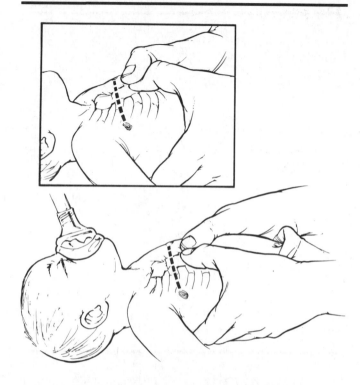

Figure 63. Hand position for chest encirclement technique for external chest compressions in neonates. Thumbs are side-by-side over the midsternum. In the small newborn, thumbs may need to be superimposed.

phase should be smooth, not jerky, and equal in time to the relaxation phase. The thumbs or fingers should not be lifted off the sternum during the relaxation phase. The pulse rate should be checked periodically and chest compressions discontinued when the spontaneous heart rate reaches 80 beats/min or greater. Compressions should always be accompanied by positive-pressure ventilations with 100% oxygen at a rate of 40–60 breaths/min.

Summary

The causes and prevention of cardiopulmonary arrest in the pediatric age group have been discussed. The distinctions among infant, child, and adult CPR have been highlighted. The sequence of actions in infant and child CPR and the management techniques for foreign body airway obstruction have been listed and described.

References

1. Seidel JS, Hornbein M, Yoshiyama K, et al: Emergency medical services and the pediatric patient: Are the needs being met? *Pediatrics* 1984;73:769.
2. Ludwig S, Kettrick RG, Parker M: Pediatric cardiopulmonary resuscitation. *Clin Pediatr* 1984;23:71.
3. Torphy DE, Minter MG, Thompson BM: Cardiorespiratory arrest and resuscitation of children. *AJDC* 1984;138:1099.
4. Statistical Resources Branch, Division of Vital Statistics: Final Mortality Statistics, 1981. Department of Health and Human Services, Public Health Service, National Center for Health Statistics. Hyattsville, MD 1984.
5. National Center for Health Statistics, DHHS, Hyattsville, Md, unpublished data.
6. Statistical Resources Branch, Division of Vital Statistics: *Final Mortality Statistics, 1981.* DHHS, Public Health Service, National Center for Health Statistics, Hyattsville, Md, 1984.
7. United States Select Panel for the Promotion of Child Health: *Better Health for Our Children: A National Strategy,* vol 1. The report to the United States Congress and the Secretary of HHS, DHHS, Public Health Service, 1981, p 79.
8. Ruben H, Elam JO, Ruben AM, Greene DG: Investigation of upper airway problems in resuscitation. *Anesthesiology* 1961;22:271.
9. Melker R: Asynchronous and other alternative methods of ventilation during CPR. *Ann Emerg Med* 1984;13(Part 2):758.
10. Melker RJ, Banner MJ: Ventilation during CPR: Two rescuer standards reappraised. *Ann Emerg Med* 1985;14:397.
11. Cavallaro D, Melker R: Comparison of two techniques for determining cardiac activity in infants. *Crit Care Med* 1983;11:189.
12. Babbs CF: New versus old theories of blood flow during CPR. *Crit Care Med* 1980;8:191.
13. Rudikoff MT, Maughan WC, Effron M, et al: Mechanism of blood flow during cardiopulmonary resuscitation. *Circulation* 1980;61:345.
14. Werner JA, Greene H, Janko CL, Cobb LA: Visualization of cardiac valve motion during external chest compression using two-dimensional echocardiography. Implications regarding the mechanism of blood flow. *Circulation* 1981; 63:1417.
15. Maier GW, Tyson GS, Olsen CO, et al: The physiology of external cardiac massage: High impulse cardiopulmonary resuscitation. *Circulation* 1984; 70:86.
16. Koehler RC, Michael JR, Guerci AD, et al: Beneficial effects of epinephrine infusion on cerebral and myocardial blood flows during CPR. *Ann Emerg Med* 1985;14:744.
17. Orlowski JP: Optimal position for external cardiac massage in infants and children. *Crit Care Med* 1984;12:224.
18. Harris CS, Baker SP, Smith GA, Harris RM: Childhood asphyxiation by food. A national analysis and overview. *JAMA* 1984;251:2231.
19. Day RL, Crelin ES, Dubois AB: Choking: The Heimlich abdominal thrust vs. back blows. An approach to measurement of inertial and aerodynamic forces. *Pediatrics* 1982;70:113.
20. Day RL, Dubois AB: Treatment of choking. *Pediatrics* 1983;71:300.
21. Day RL: Differing opinions on the emergency treatment of choking. *Pediatrics* 1983;71:976.
22. Heimlich HJ: A life-saving maneuver to prevent food choking. *JAMA* 1975;234:398.
23. Standards and Guidelines for Cardiopulmonary Resuscitation (CPR) and Emergency Cardiac Care (ECC) *JAMA* 1980;244:475.
24. Visintine RE, Baick CH: Ruptured stomach after Heimlich maneuver. *JAMA* 1975;234:415.
25. Palmer E: The Heimlich maneuver misused. *Current Prescribing* 1979; 5:45.

Special Techniques, Special Resuscitation Situations, Pitfalls, and Complications

Chapter 9

If CPR is performed improperly or inadequately, external chest compressions and rescue breathing may be ineffective in supporting life. Even properly performed CPR may result in complications.[1-4] This chapter presents important points to remember in the use of special techniques, the management of unusual situations, and the potential pitfalls and complications related to the performance of rescue breathing and chest compressions.

Special Techniques

In Two-Rescuer CPR

BLS courses for healthcare providers must include the techniques of mouth-to-mask rescue breathing and should include the cricoid pressure technique. These techniques are routinely used in many settings, are safe if performed properly, and offer some advantages in a resuscitation situation. However, they both require two rescuers for proper performance.

The Centers for Disease Control states that though it has not been shown that HIV is transmitted via saliva, the need for mouth-to-*mouth* resuscitation should be reduced as much as possible by making "mouthpieces, resuscitation bags, or other ventilation devices. . .available for use in areas in which the need for resuscitation is predictable."[5]

Mouth-to-Mask Rescue Breathing [6-8]

The adjunct used for this technique consists of a transparent mask with a mouthpiece with a one-way valve. The clear mask permits the rescuer to see vomitus when it occurs. The one-way valve provides diversion of the victim's exhaled gas away from the rescuer. The presence of an oxygen inlet allows the administration of supplemental oxygen during CPR; when this is available the oxygen flow should be between 5 and 30 L/min.

The user of this adjunct avoids direct contact with the victim's mouth, making the technique of assisted ventilation aesthetically more acceptable. However, the value of this technique in preventing transmission of infectious diseases is unknown. The cleaning/disinfecting of this device should be done in accordance with the guidelines of the manufacturer.

The technique recommended for the use of mouth-to-mask rescue breathing (two rescuers) is as follows:

1. Open the airway by head-tilt. Apply the rim of the mask first between the victim's lower lip and the chin, thus retracting the lower lip to keep the mouth open.

Once the mask is on the face of the victim, clamp it with both thumbs on the sides of the mask to provide a seal between the face and the mask. The index, middle, and ring fingers should grasp the lower jaw just above the angles of the mandible and apply pressure upward. The airway is maintained open by a combination of head-tilt/jaw-thrust.

2. Ventilate through the mouthpiece according to the recommendations for two-rescuer CPR: Two initial ventilations followed by one ventilation during the pause after the fifth chest compression. A tight seal is essential to prevent loss of volume during ventilation.

Cricoid Pressure (the Sellick Maneuver)

This technique consists of applying backward pressure on the cricoid cartilage against the cervical vertebra to prevent regurgitation and gastric distention during CPR.[9, 10] Cricoid pressure has been found to be effective in preventing regurgitation against esophageal pressures of up to 100 cm H_2O.[11] This technique should be applied only by healthcare providers where possible, in a two-rescuer CPR situation. Its application is simple but requires an assistant. It should be done during assisted ventilation and during attempted tracheal intubation. The technique is as follows:

1. To find the anatomical landmark, palpate the depression just below the thyroid cartilage (Adam's apple). This depression is the cricothyroid membrane; the prominence inferior to that is the cricoid cartilage.
2. Apply pressure to the anterolateral aspect of the cartilage just lateral to the midline. This pressure is applied with the first (thumb) and the second (index) fingers of either hand. A higher degree of pressure is required to prevent regurgitation than to prevent gastric distention.
3. If the technique is used during endotracheal intubation, the pressure on the cricoid should be maintained until the cuff of the endotracheal tube is inflated.

Moving a Victim

Questions are often asked about managing CPR when it is necessary to change locations or to carry a victim up or down stairs.

Changing Locations

A victim should not be moved from a cramped or busy location for convenience until effective CPR has been performed and the victim is stable or until help arrives and CPR can be performed without interruption.

Stairways

In some instances a victim has to be transported up or down a flight of stairs. It is best to perform CPR effectively at the head or the foot of the stairs and, at a predetermined signal, to interrupt CPR and move as quickly as possible to the next level where CPR can be resumed. Interruptions should not last longer than 30 seconds and should be avoided if possible.

Litters

While transferring a victim into an ambulance or other mobile emergency care unit, CPR should not be interrupted. Even as the victim is being moved to an ambulance, CPR must continue. With a low-wheeled litter the rescuer can stand alongside, maintaining the locked-arm position for compression. With a high litter or bed, the rescuer may have to kneel beside the victim on the bed or litter to gain the needed height over the victim's sternum.

CPR should not be interrupted for more than 5 seconds unless endotracheal intubation is being performed by trained individuals.

Special Resuscitation Situations

Near Drowning

The most important consequence of prolonged underwater submersion without ventilation is hypoxemia. There are five elements in the management of a near-drowning victim.

1. *Rescue from the water:* When attempting to rescue a near-drowning victim, the rescuer should get to the victim as quickly as possible, preferably with some conveyance (boat, raft, surfboard, or flotation device). The rescuer must always be aware of personal safety in attempting a rescue and should exercise caution to minimize the danger.
2. *Rescue breathing:* Initial treatment of the near-drowning victim consists of rescue breathing using the mouth-to-mouth or mouth-to-nose technique. Rescue breathing should be started as soon as possible, even before the victim is moved out of the water, into a boat, or onto a surfboard, provided it can be accomplished without undue risk to the rescuer. This is a special situation in which head-tilt with neck support may be of benefit.

   Appliances (such as a snorkel — using the mouth-to-snorkel technique) may permit specially trained rescuers to perform rescue breathing in deep water. However, rescue breathing should not be delayed for lack of such equipment if it can otherwise be provided safely; untrained rescuers should not attempt the use of such adjuncts.

If neck injury is suspected, however, the victim's neck should be supported in a neutral position (without flexion or extension), and the victim should be floated supine onto a horizontal back support before being removed from the water. If the victim must be turned, the head, neck, chest, and body should be aligned, supported, and turned as a unit to the horizontal, supine position. If artificial respiration is required, maximal head-tilt should not be used. Rescue breathing should be provided with the head maintained in a neutral position, i.e., jaw-thrust without head-tilt or chin-lift without head-tilt should be used.

3. *Foreign matter in the airway:* The need for clearing the lower airway of aspirated water has not been proven scientifically although there are anecdotal reports of clinical response to a subdiaphragmatic abdominal thrust.[12] At most, only a modest amount of water is aspirated by the majority of both freshwater and seawater drowning victims, and freshwater is rapidly absorbed from the lungs into the circulation.[13] Further, 10–12% of victims do not aspirate at all due to laryngospasm or breathholding.[13, 14] An attempt to remove water from the breathing passages by any means other than suction may be unnecessary and dangerous because it could eject gastric contents and cause aspiration.

   Since the risk:benefit ratio of a subdiaphragmatic abdominal thrust in this setting is unknown, the only time it definitely should be used is when the rescuer suspects that foreign matter is obstructing the airway or when the victim does not respond appropriately to mouth-to-mouth ventilation. Then, if necessary, CPR should be reinstituted after the Heimlich maneuver has been applied.[15–17] The Heimlich maneuver is performed on the near-drowning victim as described in the treatment of foreign body airway obstruction (unconscious supine) except that in near-drowning the victim's head should be turned sideways.

   Further investigation is needed to better define the need for, the risk of, and the timing of a subdiaphragmatic abdominal thrust in this situation.

4. *Chest compressions:* External chest compressions should not be attempted in the water unless the rescuer has had special training on techniques of in-water CPR because the brain is not perfused effectively unless the victim is maintained in the horizontal position and the back is supported. It is usually not possible to keep the victim's body horizontal and still keep the victim's head above water, in position for rescue breathing.

   On removal from the water, the victim must be assessed immediately for adequacy of circulation. The pulse may be difficult to appreciate in a near-drowning victim because of peripheral vasoconstriction and a low cardiac output. If a pulse cannot be felt, CPR should be started at once.

5. *Definitive (ALS) care:* There should be no delay in moving the victim to a life support unit where advanced life support is provided. Every submersion victim, even one who requires only minimal resuscitation and regains consciousness at the scene, should be transferred to a medical facility for follow-up care. It is imperative that life support measures be continued en route and that oxygen be administered if it is available in the transport vehicle.

Successful resuscitation with full neurological recovery has occurred in near-drowning victims with prolonged submersion in cold water.[18, 19] An absolute time limit beyond which resuscitation is not indicated has not been established. Since it is often difficult for rescuers to obtain an accurate time of submersion, attempts at resuscitation should be initiated by rescuers at the scene unless there is obvious physical evidence of death (such as putrefaction). The victim should be transported with continued CPR to an advanced life support facility where a physician can decide whether to continue resuscitation. Aggressive continued attempts at resuscitation on hospital arrival should be encouraged.

Physical Trauma

Survival from cardiac arrest due to traumatic injury is generally poor.[20-25] External chest compressions may not provide adequate circulation in the severely hypovolemic trauma arrest victim.[21] Emphasis should be placed on rapid transport of such patients to a trauma center where circulating blood volume can be restored and the underlying vascular injury corrected. Lay rescuers coming onto the scene of an accident should request help as soon as possible. If an automobile accident victim is pinned, the untrained lay rescuer should not attempt to move the victim unless there is further imminent danger to life, such as fire. The unconscious trauma victim should be assessed and treated using the ABCs of CPR, taking care to protect the cervical spine and attempting to control any obvious severe bleeding with direct manual compression of the wound.

In trauma victims, it is imperative that caution be used to avoid inflicting further injury by backward tilt of the head when there is a possibility of cervical spine fracture. Cervical spine fracture should be suspected in any patient with a) an injury above the clavicle or a head injury resulting in an unconscious state or b) a mechanism of injury which may have subjected the spine to sudden acceleration or deceleration (diving, fall, automobile crash, airplane crash).

If cervical spine fracture is suspected, all forward, backward, lateral, or head-turning movement should be avoided. If turning is necessary, the head, neck, chest, and body should be supported and turned as a unit. Jaw-thrust without head-tilt or chin-lift without head-tilt should be used to open the airway.

The different agencies involved in teaching rescue techniques to laypersons should have a coordinated effort for standardization and simplification of first aid techniques and should include basic CPR and special techniques for the trauma victim (hemorrhage control, positioning the unconscious victim, positioning the victim in shock, special techniques for airway control and ventilation, etc.)

Electric Shock

Complications that may follow an electric shock depend largely on the amplitude and duration of contact with the current. Electrical burns and injuries caused by falling may require prompt attention. The prognosis for victims of electric shock is not readily predictable since the amplitude and duration of the charge usually are not known. Failure of either respiration or circulation is likely to result.

It is critically important that the rescuer be certain that rescue efforts will not put him or her in danger of electrical shock. After safely clearing a victim from an energized object, the rescuer should determine the victim's cardiopulmonary status immediately. If spontaneous respiration or circulation is absent, the sequence of CPR steps should be commenced forthwith.

In cases where electric shock occurs in a location that is not readily accessible, as on a public utility pole, rescue breathing should be started at once. The victim must therefore be lowered to the ground as quickly as possible. CPR is effective only when performed on a victim who is in the horizontal position.

Lightning acts as a massive DC countershock, depolarizing the entire myocardium at once, following which the heart's normal rhythm may resume. The patients most likely to die from lightning injury are those who suffer immediate cardiac arrest.[26] Patients who do not arrest immediately have an excellent chance of recovery. Therefore, when multiple victims are simultaneously struck by lightning, individuals who appear clinically dead immediately following the strike should be treated before other victims showing signs of life.

Hypothermia

Severe accidental hypothermia (below 30° Celsius) is associated with marked depression in cerebral blood flow and oxygen requirement, reduced cardiac output, and decreased arterial pressure. Victims can appear to be clinically dead due to marked depression of brain function. Peripheral pulses may be difficult to detect because of bradycardia and vasoconstriction.

If the victim is not breathing, rescue breathing should be started. Chest compressions are indicated in the pulseless, unmonitored, suspected hypothermia victim in the field, but a longer time to check for a pulse (up to 1 minute) may be necessary.[27]

The victim should be transported with continued CPR as quickly as possible to an advanced life support treatment facility. It is important to prevent further heat loss from the core by insulating the victim and adding heat (if possible) by applying external warm objects (hot water bottles, warm packs, etc.) and/or warm, moist oxygen.[28]

BLS in Late Pregnancy

The dramatic changes in women's anatomy and physiology induced during pregnancy are of such magnitude that significant restraints must be imposed on rescuers during resuscitation of these women. The rescuer should be aware of these changes in order to anticipate problems and make appropriate modifications in CPR techniques, thus better serving both the mother and the fetus.

Before the 24th week of pregnancy, i.e., the fetal age for viability, the objectives of CPR are directed toward maternal survival. After the 24th week of pregnancy, mother and fetus are both focuses of resuscitation attempts.

During pregnancy there is a progressive increase in oxygen uptake (20–30% higher than the nonpregnant uptake) to meet the requirements of the fetus, the uterus, and the increased respiratory and cardiac work. Because of the upward displacement of the diaphragm, the functional residual capacity (FRC) of the lungs is reduced by 20%; and the oxygen reserve in the FRC is further reduced when the mother is supine.[29] This increase in oxygen demand with decrease in oxygen reserve makes the pregnant woman very sensitive to the lack of oxygen during airway obstruction, which increases the urgency for relief of the obstruction.

Another anatomical change with significant implication for CPR is compression, by the enlarged uterus, of the abdominal aorta[30] and vein (inferior vena cava). This compression of the large artery and vein will decrease the blood flow to the fetus and the venous return to the heart. External chest compressions will generate low flow and pressure during late pregnancy; if the uterus is evacuated by cesarean section, then there is a significant increase in pressure.[31] To decrease the effects of the enlarged uterus on circulation when the mother is in a supine position (as during CPR), the uterus should be displaced to the left side. This may be accomplished by:

- Having an assistant manually displace the uterus to the left side
- Placing a wedge under the right hip of the mother [32, 33] or
- Placing a folded towel under the hip [34]

There are several factors that during late pregnancy will increase the danger of vomiting and aspirating gastric contents into the lungs during resuscitation:

- Stomach emptying is delayed[35]
- The enlarged uterus causes the pressure in the stomach to increase[29]

- There is a decrease in the tonicity of the sphincter of the esophagus[29]

The rescuer should take the steps necessary to decrease the incidence of aspiration, including the application of the cricoid pressure if an extra rescuer is available who is familiar with the technique.

In the last trimester of pregnancy the uterus is above the umbilicus, which would make the application of abdominal thrusts for foreign body airway obstruction difficult. For this reason, chest thrusts are recommended.

Pitfalls and Complications

Rescue Breathing

Techniques for opening the airway should be carefully followed to avoid potential neck and spine complications. The most common reason for the inability to ventilate a patient is improper head position.

The major problem associated with excess ventilation volume and fast ventilatory flow rates is gastric distention. Rescue breathing frequently causes distention of the stomach, especially in children. This usually occurs when excessive inflation pressures are used or if the airway is partially or completely obstructed. Gastric distention can be minimized by maintaining an open airway, limiting ventilation volumes to the point at which the chest rises, and not exceeding esophageal opening pressures. Other techniques have been reported to prevent gastric distention:

1. Mouth-to-nose ventilation.[36] The rationale for this recommendation is that the nose, by providing greater resistance to the flow of ventilating gases, will decrease the pressure of the gases reaching the pharynx.
2. Slow inflation time during ventilation.[36, 37] The slower inspiratory flow rates will produce less pressure in the pharynx and thereby minimize the risk of gastric distention.
3. Cricoid pressure. This technique is described in "Special Techniques" earlier in this chapter.

Marked distention of the stomach may promote regurgitation and reduce lung volume by elevation of the diaphragm. If the stomach becomes distended during rescue breathing, recheck and reposition the airway, observe the rise and fall of the chest, and avoid excessive airway pressure. Continue rescue breathing without attempting to expel the stomach contents. Experience has shown that attempting to relieve stomach distention by manual pressure over the victim's upper abdomen is almost certain to cause regurgitation if the stomach is full. If regurgitation does occur, turn the victim's entire body to the side, wipe out the mouth, return the body to the supine position, and continue CPR.

If severe gastric distention results in inadequate ventilation, apply pressure over the epigastrium after placing the victim on the side to expel the air from the stomach. This maneuver may be necessary despite the risk of inducing regurgitation and aspiration. The use of suction by trained individuals will minimize aspiration in this situation.

Continuous pressure should not be maintained on the abdomen to help prevent gastric distention because of the danger of trapping the liver, possibly causing liver rupture (Figure 63).[38, 39] An additional reason to avoid such pressure is the possibility of regurgitation and aspiration of gastric contents.

External Chest Compressions

Care should be taken to adhere to the recommendations concerning external chest compression techniques. Pulselessness must be established prior to performing compressions. Proper CPR techniques lessen the possibilities of complications resulting from improperly performed compressions.

Even properly performed external chest compressions can cause rib fractures in some patients. Other complications that may occur despite proper CPR techniques include fracture of the sternum, separation of the ribs from the sternum, pneumothorax, hemothorax, lung contusions, lacerations of the liver and spleen, and fat emboli. These complications may be minimized by careful attention to details of performance, but they cannot be entirely prevented. Accordingly, concern for injuries that may result even from properly performed CPR should not impede prompt and energetic application of the technique. The only alternative to timely initiation of effective CPR for the cardiac arrest victim is death.

Improper hand position for external chest compressions should be avoided by careful identification of landmarks. Applying pressure too low on the chest may cause the tip of the sternum to cut into the liver and cause internal bleeding (Figure 64).

The rescuer's fingers should not rest on the victim's ribs during compression. Interlocking the fingers of the rescuer's hands may help avoid this. Pressure with fingers on the ribs or lateral (sideways) pressure increases

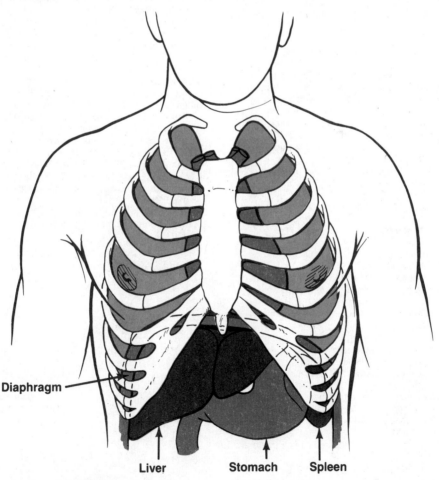

Figure 64. Intra-abdominal organs in relation to chest anatomy.

Diaphragm

Liver   Stomach   Spleen

the possibility of rib fractures and costochondral separations. Between compressions, the heel of the hand must completely release its pressure but should remain in constant contact with the chest wall over the lower half of the sternum.

Compressions should be smooth, regular, and uninterrupted except for rescue breathing. There should be equal compression and relaxation cycles. Sudden or jerking movements should be avoided. Jabs can increase the possibility of injury to the ribs and internal organs and may decrease the amount of blood circulated by each compression. The lower half of the sternum of an adult must be depressed about 1½–2 inches (3.8–5 cm) during each chest compression. Less depth of compression may be ineffective.

Summary

Complications and problems with the effective administration of CPR can be lessened by adhering to the techniques described in Chapters 4 and 8 and the proper sequences described in Chapters 5 through 7. Even properly applied CPR may result in complications, but failure to attempt resuscitation most surely will result in death for the victim.

References

1. Nagel EL, Fine EG, Krischer JP, et al: Complications of CPR. *Crit Care Med* 1981;9:424.
2. Elam JD, Sterling R: Airway management. I. M-A-S: A mouth mask–airway–sump system for upper airway control. II. Elastometeric cuffs for long-dwelling endotracheal tubes. *Crit Care Med* 1981;9:425.
3. Bjork RJ, Snyder BD, Campion DC, et al: Medical complications of cardiopulmonary arrest. *Arch Intern Med* 1982;142:500–503.
4. Atcheson SG, Fred HL: Complications of cardiac resuscitation. (letter) *Am Heart J* 1975;89:263–264.
5. Centers for Disease Control: Recommendations for prevention of HIV transmission in health-care settings. *MMWR* 1987;36(suppl 2):2S.
6. Elam JO, Brown ES, Elder JD Jr: Artificial respiration by mouth-to-mask method. A study of the respiratory gas exchange of paralyzed patients ventilated by the operator's expired air. *N Engl J Med* 1954;250:749–754.
7. Safar P: Packet mask for emergency artificial ventilation and oxygen inhalation. *Crit Care Med* 1974;2:273,274.
8. Harrison RR, Maull KI, Kwwnan RL, et al: Mouth-to-mask ventilation: A superior method of rescue breathing. *Ann Emerg Med* 1982;11:74,75.
9. Keith A: Mechanism underlying the various methods of artificial respiration. *Lancet* Mar 13, 1909, p 747.
10. Sellick BA: Cricoid pressure to control regurgitation of stomach contents during induction of anesthesia. *Lancet* 1961;2:404–406.
11. Salem MR, Wong AY, Mani M, et al: Efficacy of cricoid pressure in preventing gastric distention during bag-mask ventilation in pediatric patients. *Anesthesiology* 1974;40:96–98.
12. Heimlich HJ: Subdiaphragmatic pressure to expel water from the lungs of drowning persons. *Ann Emerg Med* 1981;10:476–480.
13. Modell JH, Davis JH: Electrolyte changes in human drowning victims. *Anesthesiology* 1969;30:414–420.
14. Modell JH: Is the Heimlich maneuver appropriate as first treatment for drowning? *Emerg Med Serv* 1981;10:63–66.
15. Patrick EA: The Heimlich maneuver. *Emergency* 1981;13:45–47.
16. Heimlich HJ: The Heimlich maneuver: First treatment for drowning victims. *Emerg Med Serv* 1981;10:58–61.
17. Heimlich HJ: Editorial commentary. *Emerg Med Serv* 1982;11:93–96.
18. Siebke H, Rod T, Breivik H, et al: Survival after 40 minutes submersion without cerebral sequelae. *Lancet* 1975;1:1275–1277.
19. Southwick FS, Dalglish PH: Recovery after prolonged asystolic cardiac arrest in profound hypothermia. A case report and literature review. *JAMA* 1980;243:1250–1253.
20. Baker CC, Thomas AN, Trunkey DD: The role of emergency room thoracotomy in trauma. *J Trauma* 1980;20:848–855.
21. Mattox KL, Feliciano DV: Role of external cardiac compression in truncal trauma. *J Trauma* 1982;22:934–936.
22. Vij D, Simoni E, Smith RF, et al: Resuscitative thoracotomy for patients with traumatic injury. *Surgery* 1983;94:554–561.
23. Shimazu S, Shatney CH: Outcomes of trauma patients with no vital signs on hospital admission. *J Trauma* 1983;23:213–216.
24. Cogbill TH, Moore EE, Millikan JS, et al: Rationale for selective application of emergency department thoracotomy in trauma. *J Trauma* 1983;23: 453–460.
25. Flynn TC, Ward RE, Miller PW: Emergency department thoracotomy. *Ann Emerg Med* 1982;11:413–416.
26. Cooper MA: Lightning injuries: Prognostic signs for death. *Ann Emerg Med* 1980;9:134–138.
27. Steinman AM: The hypothermic code: CPR controversy revisited. *J Emerg Med Serv* 1983;10:32–35.
28. Samuelson T, Doolittle W, Hayward J, et al: Hypothermia and cold water near drowning: Treatment guidelines. *Alaska Med* 1982;24:106–111.
29. Gibbs CP: Maternal physiology. *Clin Obstet Gynecol* 1981;24:525–543.
30. Bieniarz J, Crottogini JJ, Curuchet E, et al: Aortocaval compression by the uterus in late pregnancy. *Am J Obstet Gynecol* 1968;100:203–217.
31. DePace NL, Betesh JS, Kotler MN: Postmortem cesarean section with recovery of both mother and offspring. *JAMA* 1982;248:971–973.
32. Eckstein KL, Marx GF: Aortocaval compression and uterine displacement. *Anesthesiology* 1974;40:92–96.
33. Colon-Morales MA: Self-supporting device for continuous left uterine displacement during cesarean section. *Anesth Analg* 1970;49:223–224.
34. Marx GF, Bassell GM: Hazards of the supine position in pregnancy. *Clin Obstet Gynecol* 1982;9:255–271.
35. LaSalvia LA, Steffen EA: Delayed gastric emptying time in labor. *Am J Obstet Gynecol* 1950;59:1075–1081.
36. Ruben H, Elam JO, Ruben AM, et al: Investigation of upper airway problems in resuscitation. *Anesthesiology* 1961;22:271–279.
37. Melker R: Asynchronous and other alternative methods of ventilation during CPR. *Ann Emerg Med* 1984;13(pt 2):758–761.
38. Wilder RJ, Weir D, Rush BE, et al: Methods of coordinating ventilation and closed-chest cardiac massage in the dog. *Surgery* 1963;53:186–194.
39. Harris LC, Kirimli B, Safar P: Augmentation of artificial circulation during cardiopulmonary resuscitation. *Anesthesiology* 1967;28:730–734.

Chapter 10

CPR Safety for Learners, Instructors, and Rescuers

This chapter addresses concerns commonly expressed by students of cardiopulmonary resuscitation (CPR) and their instructors — as well as rescuers participating in actual resuscitations. This information should help answer questions relevant to disease transmission and rescuer safety.

The following topics are included:

- Disease transmission during CPR training and performance
- Rescuer safety during CPR training

New information regarding these topics emerges regularly. Instructors and students should familiarize themselves with more current data and information as they become available.

Disease Transmission During CPR

Much concern has recently been raised about the risk to the rescuer of contracting infectious diseases by participating in CPR training or by performing CPR on circulatory and/or respiratory arrest victims. In view of this concern and the continuing public health need for CPR training and prompt availability, the following recommendations are made, based on the latest scientific information and advice from the Centers for Disease Control (CDC) in Atlanta.

CPR Training

The risk of transmission of any infectious disease by manikin practice appears to be minimal to negligible. In fact, while an estimated 40 million people in the U.S. and perhaps 150 million worldwide have been taught mouth-to-mouth rescue breathing on manikins in the last 25 years, there has never been a documented case of transmission of bacterial, fungal, or viral disease by a CPR training manikin.

If the AHA, American Red Cross, and CDC recommendations for cleaning and maintaining manikins are consistently followed, the students of each CPR training class should be presented with manikins having a sanitary quality equal to or better than eating utensils in a properly operated restaurant. To assure this high level of safety, it is imperative that all Instructors and Course Directors follow precisely the recommendations outlined below on cleaning and maintaining manikins. If two-person rescue is practiced, the second student should simulate ventilation instead of blowing into the manikin. Finally, the finger sweep maneuver to relieve a foreign body obstruction should be simulated or, if performed on a manikin, the airway of the manikin should be decontaminated before the procedure and again after the procedure.

Performance of CPR

The vast majority of CPR performed in the United States is done by healthcare and public safety personnel, many of whom perform mouth-to-mouth ventilation frequently throughout the year on cardiac arrest victims about whom they have little or no medical information. A layperson is less likely to be in a situation to perform CPR than is a healthcare provider. A layperson who performs CPR is most likely to do so in the home, commonly knows the cardiac arrest victim, and often has prior knowledge of the victim's health. The greatest concern over the theoretical risk of disease transmission from mouth-to-mouth resuscitation should be directed at individuals who perform CPR frequently, such as healthcare providers and public safety personnel.

Clear plastic face masks with one-way valves are available for use in mouth-to-mask ventilation; they divert the victim's exhaled gas away from the rescuer. Healthcare providers and public safety personnel who have been properly trained in their use may use these masks rather than the mouth-to-mouth technique. (Mouth-to-mask training does not replace, but is in addition to, the required mouth-to-mouth training.) The need for and effectiveness of this adjunct in preventing the transmission of infectious diseases during mouth-to-mask ventilation is not known. This sort of device may be used to reassure the rescuer that a potential risk may thus be minimized, but the rescuer must be adequately trained in its use, especially in making an adequate face-to-mask seal and maintaining a patent airway. Since it requires two hands to make a face-to-mask seal and maintain an open airway, this device should be used only when there are two rescuers performing the CPR. The masks should be cleaned and disinfected after each use, using the methods described for decontaminating CPR training manikins. As an additional precaution, rescuers may elect to wear latex gloves since saliva or blood on the victim's mouth or face may be transferred to the rescuer's hands.

In 1985 there was a dramatic increase in the number of inquiries to the Centers for Disease Control regarding the adequacy of current manikin-decontamination recommendations for killing the viral agent of acquired immunodeficiency syndrome (AIDS). Recent studies have shown that the retroviral agent that causes AIDS, human immunodeficiency virus (HIV), is comparatively delicate and is inactivated in less than 10 minutes at room temperature by a number of chemicals, including the agents (and concentrations) recommended for manikin decontamination — alcohol or sodium hypochlorite (household bleach).[1] Coupled with soap and water (scrubbing and rinsing), the recommended sodium hypochlorite dilution will assure that the HIV virus as well as a wide variety of other infectious agents will be killed. A higher level of surface disinfection is not warranted; the recommended disinfectants (alcohol or household bleach) are safe, effective, inexpensive, easily obtained, and well tolerated by students, Instructors, and manikin surfaces when properly used. Current research and recommendations for preventing HIV contamination on surfaces emphasize that there is no evidence to date that AIDS is transmitted by casual personal contact, by indirect contact with inanimate surfaces, or by an airborne virus.

In the absence of evidence of risk from infectious diseases, including AIDS, the life-saving potential of CPR should continue to be vigorously emphasized, and energetic efforts in support of broadscale CPR training should be continued.

Rescuer Safety During CPR Training

Some CPR learners are at risk for other than cross-contamination problems. Individuals with certain medical conditions and health problems may experience difficulty acquiring these skills. Because of the nature of the psychomotor skills development during CPR training and the requisite physical exertion, these individuals may not learn the skills of CPR at the same pace as healthy learners. Further, these individuals may find the required exertion unsafe in that certain conditions may become aggravated as a result of skills practice.

An estimated 10% of all CPR learners will present some history or condition that may affect their ability to perform CPR. These individuals are generally not considered disabled because the impairment does not impede performance of daily activities and society does not consider them disabled. Examples reported in the literature include learners with histories of myocardial infarction, allergic reactions to manikins, angina, hypoglycemia, arthritis, asthma, hypertension, various breathing disorders, diabetes, and back problems. Other problems that had a direct adverse effect on CPR learners' skills development included arm surgery that prevented full extension during compression and head and neck surgery with residual mouth distortion that prevented the learner from making an adequate mouth-to-mouth seal.

In addition, Instructors relate experiences with learners whose conditions cause them (and the Instructor) to need additional time, practice, patience, and guidance. These conditions include

- Obesity
- Smoking
- Poor general physical condition
- Dentures

There is no single, specific solution to help these learners overcome these physical disabilities except additional practice time and patience. However, the need for additional time may itself aggravate some of these existing health problems. Instructors must therefore balance practice time with rest periods and observe learners closely for signs of fatigue during actual practice.

Instructors also report several other problems that come about as a result of CPR manikin practice. These include a) light-headedness during ventilation practice, b) circumoral bruises after ventilation practice, c) thenar eminence blisters on the dominant compression hand, and d) pressure bruises on top of the hand after compressions. Advising learners of these potential problems and helping them to pace their practice to avoid such problems will usually prevent their occurrence. Instructors may still need to intervene and advise the overenthusiastic learners to take rest periods and pace themselves during manikin practice.

The physical stress required of the learner during CPR practice has been assessed. It was found that only a submaximal physical effort was required by healthy rescuers to perform good CPR as measured by heart rate and total body oxygen consumption (VO_2).[2] However, the effect was enough to generate a mean rescuer rate pressure product (RPP) approaching 20,000. These data suggest that CPR might elicit ischemic symptoms in a rescuer with coronary artery disease. However, it was also found that CPR practice is more comparable to submaximal exercise and is performed under a constant load rather than an increasing load. Energy expenditure during CPR by healthy performers is also submaximal.

There are data that suggest that individuals with preexisting conditions may experience aggravation of these problems. Instructors should advise all CPR learners about the level of physical activity involved and help them to pace their practice according to individual ability.

The life-saving benefit of this instruction far outweighs any reason to deny access to CPR instruction to any individual who wants to acquire these skills.

References

1. Centers for Disease Control: Guidelines for prevention of transmission of human immunodeficiency virus and hepatitis B virus to health-care and public safety workers. *MMWR* 1989;38(suppl 6):1–37.
2. Lonergan J: Cardiopulmonary resuscitation: Physical stress on the rescuer. *Crit Care Med* 9:793-795, 1981.

Supplemental Bibliography

Bond WW. Inactivation of AIDS virus in clothing (question-answer). *JAMA* 253:258, 1985.

Greenberg, M: CPR: A report of observed medical complications during training. *Ann Emerg Med* 12:194–195, 1983.

Lettau LA, Bond WW, McDougal JS: Hepatitis and a diaphragm fitting (letter). *JAMA* 254:752, 1985.

MacCauley C, Todd C: Physical disability among cardiopulmonary resuscitation students. *Occupational Health Nurs* 3:17–19, 1978.

Martin LS, McDougal JS, Loskoski SL. Disinfection and inactivation of the human T Lymphotrophic virus Type III/Lymphadenopathy-Associated Virus. *J Infect Dis* 152:400–403, 1985.

McDougal JS, Cort SP, Kennedy MS, et al: Immunoassay for detection and quantitation of infectious viral particles of the human retrovirus Lymphadenopathy-Associated Virus (LAV). *J Immunol Methods* 76:171–193, 1985.

Memon A, Salyer J, Hillman E, Marshall C: Fatal myocardial infarction following CPR training: The question of risk. *Ann Emerg Med* 11:322–323, 1982.

Salyer J, Marshall C, Hillman E, Boyle J, Bullock J: Letter to editor. *Ann Emerg Med* 12:195, 1983.

Spire B, Dormont D, Barre-Simoussi F, et al: Interactivation of Lymphadenopathy-Associated Virus by Heat, Gamma Rays and Ultraviolet Light. *Lancet* 6:188–189, 1985.

Appendix A: Medicolegal Considerations and Decision-Making in CPR

A goal of the American Heart Association is to assure that the standards and guidelines for cardiopulmonary resuscitation and emergency cardiac care are the best possible based on scientific knowledge and medical practice. Legal liability may be based on either the quality of the care delivered or the decision to provide, withhold, or withdraw care.[1] Delivering high quality care while maintaining sensitivity to the emotional needs and realities of patients and those close to them is the best way for care providers to avoid legal action.

The following medicolegal/ethical principles were formulated to help enhance the quality of care provided while protecting the patient's right to accept or reject therapy and to clarify the physician's role in making decisions to provide, withhold, or withdraw life support:

1. Individuals to whom a duty of care is owed should receive the appropriate care, and arbitrary bases for decisions to withhold care should be avoided.
2. Individuals who, when competent, would have preferred to have resuscitative efforts withheld or withdrawn under certain circumstances should have the benefit of mechanisms by which these desires can be accomplished when they are not competent.
3. The physician unable to determine to his or her satisfaction what the patient, when competent, would have chosen should have guidance as to an approach consistent with both the patient's rights and the physician's professional obligations.
4. Prospective decision-making by individuals in anticipation of their becoming incompetent should be encouraged so as to optimize the role of the patient in decisions that affect his or her life and death.
5. The special medicolegal aspects of CPR and ECC in children should be recognized and considered.

Because of the strong implications of the terms "standards," "guidelines," and "successful course completion," both medically and legally, clarification of what they are intended to convey herein is of prime importance. The evolution of their meanings in the context of CPR/ECC, their definitions for this publication, and equally important, what they do *not* mean are discussed in the following section.

Definition and Intent of Standards and Guidelines

The term "standards" was employed in the 1974 *JAMA* supplement on standards in CPR and ECC because previously there had not been a body of information that reflected the state of the art in BLS and ACLS. Virtually complete acceptance of the recommendations and concepts in the 1974 standards resulted in the development of BLS teaching materials by different agencies, particularly the American Red Cross and the AHA, that were for the most part consistent, thus minimizing the possibilities for confusion.

The title for the 1980 *JAMA* publication was "Standards and Guidelines for Cardiopulmonary Resuscitation (CPR) and Emergency Cardiac Care (ECC)," with "standards" meant to apply to BLS teaching, especially as it referred to laypersons, while "standards" or "guidelines" were used interchangeably with reference to ACLS.

The 1980 standards and guidelines were intended to

1. Identify a body of knowledge and certain performance skills that are commonly necessary for the successful treatment of victims of cardiorespiratory arrest or other serious or life-threatening cardiac or pulmonary disturbances
2. Indicate that the knowledge and skills recommended or defined do not represent the only medically or legally acceptable approach to a designated problem but rather an approach that is generally regarded as having the best likelihood of success in view of present knowledge
3. Provide a uniform basis for teaching, testing, and maintaining quality in BLS and ACLS on a local and national level
4. Stimulate the widest possible dissemination not only of the knowledge and performance skills of BLS but also of the knowledge of risk reduction and primary prevention, to the largest number of persons possible
5. Provide, to the extent possible, a single approach to the performance of BLS to the public

The standards and guidelines were NOT intended to imply

1. That justifiable deviations from suggested standards and guidelines by physicians qualified and experienced in CPR and ECC under appropriate circumstances represent a breach of a medical standard of care
2. That new knowledge, techniques, clinical or research data, clinical experience, or clinical circumstances may not provide sound reasons for alternative approaches to CPR and ECC before the next definition of national standards and guidelines

The words "certified" or "certification" are not used to describe completion of the BLS course or the document issued for successful completion of the course. The American Heart Association does not purport to warrant future BLS performance by a Provider or to provide a license of any type for completion of the course.

Decision-Making: Providing, Withholding, and Withdrawing Life Support

The decision-making process in medicine has evolved dramatically over the past 20 years. Until the 1950's the physician's recommendation was almost always the determining factor in important medical decisions. As the number and complexity of medical options and the capacity to control life and death expanded in the sixties and seventies, so did the number, complexity, and cost of lawsuits against medical practitioners. The courts became increasingly protective of the individual's right to self-determination. The potential for tension between the physician and the patient and family increased. The physician was driven by the need to provide care, but the courts increasingly emphasized the patient's right to accept or refuse care as that individual patient so desired. An understanding of the contemporary medicolegal setting is helpful in approaching the difficult problem of decision-making in life-and-death situations and in providing a method for observing the patient's rights while providing high-quality emergency care and preserving the physician's integrity and responsibility.

The physician is trained to preserve, protect, and prolong life and to act aggressively, if necessary, to achieve these ends. The goals of hospitals have been the same. While both hospitals and physicians are aware of the rights of patients in the decision-making process, the physician may be disconcerted by the prospect of not being permitted to provide care, because of patient refusal, when the life-threatening process is potentially reversible. This situation generates conflict for physicians as well as other healthcare providers. The problem of life-and-death decision-making becomes all the more difficult when the patient is incompetent and there is no legally empowered decision-maker. This circumstance forces the question when or whether the courts should be involved, especially when the medical context is emergency cardiac care.

In addition, patient "refusal" of care, including the existence of a living will, may make it more difficult to evolve a coherent plan of care for the patient once the decision not to resuscitate has been reached and the do-not-resuscitate (DNR) order has been recorded. Clarification of the medicolegal decision-making process is of critical importance in terms of both human and medical costs. It may be the single most pressing challenge in the areas of CPR, ECC, and critical care in general.

An Obligation to Provide CPR

When a physician-patient relationship exists, the physician has an obligation to initiate CPR when medically indicated and when DNR status is not in force. Similarly, when nurses or paramedical persons are functioning in their official capacities, they have a positive obligation to initiate CPR when it is indicated. (In most states, the nurse and paramedic have been included in immunity statutes intended to protect them from liability for performing CPR out of the professional setting.)

Thus, the accepted context in which a decision to withhold CPR may be made requires first that resuscitation can and will be implemented by a responsible person or agency if two conditions are fulfilled:

1. If there is the possibility that the brain is viable
2. If there is no legal or medical reason to withhold it

The first condition is determined by defining the presence or absence of brain death. The second provides for the possibility that resuscitation might not be indicated if it could do no good or if a competent refusal of CPR has been made.

Reasons to Withhold CPR?

Death: Few reliable criteria exist by which death can be defined immediately. Decapitation, rigor mortis, and perhaps evidence of tissue decomposition and extreme dependent lividity are usually reliable criteria. When they are present, CPR need not be initiated. In the absence of such findings, CPR generally should be initiated immediately unless there is another acceptable medical or legal reason to withhold it. If the decision not to initiate CPR is made by a medical professional functioning in the professional capacity, it must be based on acceptable medical standards. The reason to withhold CPR should be sufficiently solid so that, should the decision be subject to question, it can be medically supported.

DOA (Dead on Arrival): Problems associated with the "DOA" designation have been the subject of extended discussions.[1] Delayed resuscitative efforts on behalf of victims of prehospital cardiac arrest have met with increasing success. However, one tragic outcome is the seriously brain-damaged survivor. This infrequent and unpredictable outcome has led to efforts to determine, in advance of initiation of CPR, whether the cardiac arrest victim is likely to recover fully. Such a determination is usually based on estimates of the time elapsed since the onset of cardiac arrest. The danger is that the patient's right to treatment may be compromised by the time taken to make this determination of CNS recoverability.

In any case, it is usually impossible to determine accurately the duration of complete cessation of cardiovascular function because competent and reliable observers are not usually present at the scene of collapse. To make a decision not to initiate CPR in this setting, the physician must be confident, at least, that the observer is able to recognize cardiac arrest, the observer is reliable in documenting the time elapsed, the observer is acting in good faith, and no independent influences on CNS function, such as drugs or hypothermia, are operative. The argument that the patient could have collapsed, from a cardiac or noncardiac cause, yet continued to have cardiac activity sufficient to sustain the brain until arrival at the emergency facility may be insurmountable.

A designation of "dead on arrival" should take into account the Uniform Determination of Death Act, which has been endorsed by the American Bar Association, the American Medical Association, and the National Conference of Commissioners on Uniform State Laws and adopted by some states:

> An individual who has sustained either (1) irreversible cessation of circulatory and respiratory functions or (2) irreversible cessation of all functions of the entire brain, including the brain stem, is dead. A determination of death must be made in accordance with accepted medical standards.[2]

Without testing the responsiveness of the cardiovascular system through resuscitative efforts, one is unable to judge that "irreversible cessation of circulatory and respiratory functions" has occurred. Similarly, there is no objective means for determining "irreversible cessation of all functions of the entire brain" unless circulation is reestablished. Thus, the better course of action, when doubt exists, is to assume the patient is not dead, initiate cardiopulmonary resuscitation, and deal with the outcome as a second-level issue.

Irreversible Brain Damage: Another basis for withholding CPR has been the conclusion, often reached after an examination performed at the moment the decision needs to be made, that there is evidence of irreversible brain damage. Is the suspicion of irreversible brain damage or "brain death," based on a momentary examination, a valid reason for withholding CPR?

The absence of a pupillary response to light, traditionally thought to be evidence of brain death, is not a reliable indicator, since certain diseases and drugs can render the pupil nonreactive, as can certain types of cataract surgery. Perhaps more important, initially unreactive pupils may become reactive in the course of resuscitation. The detection of "boxcars" in the fundi has been recognized as an indicator of cessation of cerebral perfusion and, therefore, of brain death. But the acceptability of this sign, assuming its validity, depends finally on the reliabilty of the observer.

Misdiagnosis of irreversible cessation of all brain function has been reported in the case of brain contusion in association with reduced cerebral function due to hypovolemia. Vigorous treatment of hypovolemic shock resulted in recovery despite that misdiagnosis.[3]

One is left with the reality that there are practically no useful, reliable signs of brain death that can be applied in a timely manner to the cardiac arrest victim, with the exception of decapitation, rigor mortis, and perhaps established dependent lividity. Therefore, since it is usually not possible to predict nonrecoverability of a brain acutely insulted by cardiac arrest, and since attempts to do so increase anoxia time and the likelihood of further permanent brain damage, the responsible physician, nurse, or paramedic is usually obligated to commence cardiopulmonary resuscitation. Evaluation of brain status and the difficult decisions that may be forthcoming in this regard should be deferred until the issue of cardiovascular responsiveness is determined. The DOA designation is in large measure an anachronism and an invitation to legal as well as medical sanctions.

Patient Refusal: A major reason for withholding CPR is the competent refusal of such treatment by the patient. A critical aspect here is the term "competent." The test of "competency" always runs the risk of a false-positive result. The greater the risk of a false-positive result, the more strongly one needs to guard against it. Thus, for the patient who is clearly in a terminal condition, the risk of a false-positive test of competency is very small indeed. When the patient's condition is not terminal and when death is not imminent but the cardiac arrest risk is real, the question of whether refusal was competent becomes much more important.

In addition, there may be some legal limitations on the right of the individual to refuse life-saving or life-prolonging treatment, i.e., the state's obligation to preserve life, the patient is pregnant, or the patient has dependent children. Certainly, the patient's right to refuse care bears importantly on the issue of DNR status.

Do Not Resuscitate (DNR) Orders: It is generally accepted that resuscitation is a form of medical therapy that, like most others, is indicated in some situations but not in others. This conviction was clearly enunciated at the National Conferences on CPR and ECC in 1974 and 1979.[4, 5] When doubt exists, however, resuscitation should be instituted.[1, 4, 5] One of the situations in which CPR is usually not indicated is in the case of the terminally ill patient for whom no further therapy for the underlying disease process remains available and for whom death appears imminent.[6] In describing an "irreversibly, irreparably ill patient whose death was imminent," the following definitions have been suggested[6]: *irreversible,* a case of no known therapeutic measures being effective in reversing the course of the illness; *irreparable,* when the course of the illness had progressed beyond the capacity of existing knowledge and technique to stem it; *imminent death,* in the ordinary course of events probably occurring within a period of two weeks. (In such a case a note summarizing the patient's condition and the basis for the decision to withhold CPR should be written on the patient's chart and the physician's order sheet.[5, 6])

Court cases have clearly supported the use of DNR orders in appropriate circumstances,[7] and recent surveys of DNR decisions have provided information on the circumstances in which these orders are used.[8–10] Yet, there are indications that DNR decisions are not being faced as frequently as they should be and that they are not fulfilling the goals for which they were intended.[8–10]

When the decision not to resuscitate is made by the patient or the patient's family and physician, it should be expressed clearly in the medical record for the benefit of nursing and other personnel who may be called on to initiate or participate in CPR. DNR orders do not and should not be interpreted to imply any other change in the level of medical or nursing care. The patient's family should understand and agree with the decision, although the family's opinion need not be controlling if the patient is competent. Physicians and the entire medical team should be in general agreement with the decision. This may be facilitated by a confirmatory written opinion from appropriate qualified consultants.

When "DNR" is written, it means do not make resuscitative efforts. If specific types of intervention are desired by the physician, they should be written specifically, i.e., "lidocaine for V.T." or, in the case of a child with severe pulmonary disease, "resuscitate short of intubation," if the prospect of life on a ventilator has been appropriately discussed and refused by the family.

Withdrawing BLS

Nonphysicians should initiate CPR to the best of their knowledge and capability in cases they recognize as cardiac arrest. Nonphysicians who initiate BLS or ACLS should continue resuscitation efforts until one of the following occurs:

1. Effective spontaneous circulation and ventilation have been restored.
2. Resuscitation efforts have been transferred to another responsible person who continues BLS.
3. A physician or a physician-directed person or team assumes responsibility.
4. The victim is transferred to properly trained personnel charged with responsibilities for emergency medical services.
5. The rescuer is exhausted and unable to continue resuscitation.

Physicians should continue resuscitative efforts until one of the following occurs:

1. The physician has reasonable assurance that the victim will continue to receive properly performed BLS, ACLS, or both.
2. The patient recovers.
3. The patient is found to be unresuscitatable (see following) and is pronounced dead.

Liability Risks of Individuals and Groups

Immunity "Good Samaritan" Laws

"Good Samaritan" laws have been expanded in a number of jurisdictions to protect almost every professional and layperson while that individual is acting "in good faith" and is not guilty of gross negligence. An important purpose of such laws is to minimize, to the greatest extent possible, fear of legal consequences for providing CPR and to eliminate effectively this fear as an impediment to full implementation of a multilevel community ECC program.

Layperson Liability for CPR

Individual Rescuers: There was no instance known to 1985 National Conference faculty and participants in which a layperson who has performed CPR reasonably has been sued successfully. There are a number of reasons why any such legal action is extremely unlikely in the future. These include:

1. The provision of statutory immunity to laypersons as well as medical professionals in many jurisdictions for performance of CPR, in the form of "Good Samaritan" laws
2. The fact that successful prosecution of a layperson performing CPR in good faith would discourage, if not terminate, future layperson CPR and thus run counter to established public policy and interest

Laypersons are protected under most "Good Samaritan" laws if they perform CPR even if they have had no formal training.

Layperson CPR is beneficial for the cardiac arrest victim when performed in accordance with recognized standards. The BLS standards herein have been altered modestly to simplify teaching and remembering, thereby enhancing the confidence of the rescuer and, thus, the effectiveness of CPR.

All citizens reasonably able to perform CPR, and for whom such performance does not pose a medical or psychoemotional danger, should be trained in and capable of performing CPR at a level to sustain the life of a respiratory and/or cardiac arrest victim until definitive therapy becomes available.

CPR Teachers and Organizations: People who are trainers in CPR are also protected under many "Good Samaritan" laws, as are organizations that sponsor this training, i.e., the American Heart Association, the American Red Cross, and similar agencies. The concern for liability for layperson CPR should not represent an impediment to full implementation of ECC capability.

Medicolegal Considerations in the Pediatric Age Group

Decision-Making for Infants and Children

The current focus of CPR emphasizes approaches to promoting self-determination by competent and incompetent adult patients. In contrast, the affected pediatric population ranges from the never-competent infant and young child under parental guardianship to the maturing adolescent with progressively expanding decisional capacity.

Recent legislative and judicial activity has been directed at attempting to strike a balance between the presumed best interests of the child, the rights of the parents, the preservation of family unity, and the recognition of age-appropriate levels of autonomy. This area of public policy is currently evolving rapidly.

Ethical and Legal Obligations

The student of basic and advanced cardiac life support must know the following about the ethical and legal obligations with respect to children that attend life-saving skills:

1. The underlying premise of a training module specifically dedicated to pediatric CPR asserts that children are different and that appropriate management regimens cannot safely be derived simply from scaled-down adult versions.

2. To the extent that American Heart Association CPR guidelines are accepted as a legal standard of care, in cases involving childhood cardiac arrest victims performance of trainees successfully completing a course will be judged against the content of the pediatric basic and advanced cardiac life support courses.

3. In addition to distinguishing clinical and technical aspects peculiar to pediatric patients, these standards also imply an appreciation of the respective rights of parents and children, the limits of parental authority, and the role of the state in protecting the welfare of children.

4. It is the responsibility of the professional to recognize when the rights of parents and children may clash in pursuit of conflicting interests, especially in the process of making decisions to withhold CPR, and to utilize available institutional and judicial resources to ensure that the best interests of the child are upheld.

5. Where there exists substantial doubt about the authority or reasonableness of guardian requests to withhold CPR, a prescription in favor of resuscitation should govern professional conduct until a resolution of conflict can be achieved.

6. Similarly, where potential rescuers are unsure of their pediatric skills, they should nevertheless undertake good faith efforts at resuscitation to the limit of their ability, relying on legal protection based on common law doctrines or Good Samaritan statutes.

7. Mechanisms need to be established to allow parents to make judgments that are in the best interests of their children and that can be guided by principles such as those laid out by the American Medical Association's Judicial Council.[11]

References

1. McIntyre KM: Medicolegal aspects of decision-making in resuscitation and life support. *Cardiovasc Rev Rep* 1983;4:46–56.
2. Guidelines for the determination of death. *JAMA* 1981;246:2184.
3. Grenvik A, Powner DJ, Snyder JV, et al: Cessation of therapy in terminal illness and brain death. *Crit Care Med* 1978;6:284–291.
4. Standards for Cardiopulmonary Resuscitation (CPR) and Emergency Cardiac Care (ECC). *JAMA* 1974;227(suppl):833–868.
5. Standards and Guidelines for Cardiopulmonary Resuscitation (CPR) and Emergency Cardiac Care (ECC). *JAMA* 1980;244(suppl):453–509.
6. Rabkin MT, Gillerman G, Rice NR: Orders not to resuscitate. *N Engl J Med* 1976;295:364–366.
7. In re Dinnerstein, 380 NE2d 134 (Mass App 1978).
8. Bedell SE, Delbanco TL: Choices about cardiopulmonary resuscitation in the hospital. When do physicians talk with patients? *N Engl J Med* 1984; 310(17):1089–1092.
9. Lo B, Saika G, Strill W, et al: "Do Not Resuscitate" decisions. A prospective study of three teaching hospitals. *Arch Int Med* 1985;145:1115–1117.
10. Evans AL, Brody BA: The do-not-resuscitate order in teaching hospitals. *JAMA* 1985;253(15):2236–2239.
11. Current opinions of the Judicial Council of the American Medical Association, 1984.

Appendix B: Course C Curriculum and Completion Criteria

Module/Curriculum	Written Test	Performance Test

1. Adult One-Rescuer CPR
Heart and lung function
Risk factors
Prudent heart living
Signals of heart attack
Actions for survival
One-rescuer CPR
2. Adult FBAO Management
Conscious
Conscious becomes unconscious
Unconscious
3. Pediatric One-Rescuer CPR
Risk factors/prevention
Child one-rescuer CPR
Infant CPR
4. Pediatric FBAO Management
Infant obstructed airway
  conscious
  conscious becomes unconscious
  unconscious
Child obstructed airway
  conscious
  conscious becomes unconscious
  unconscious
5. Adult Two-Rescuer CPR
6. Child Two-Rescuer CPR
**7. Mouth-to-Mask Ventilation
and Cricoid Pressure** (optional)
	Risk factors, adult
	Prudent heart living
	Signals of heart attack
	Actions for survival
	Adult one-rescuer CPR
	Adult two-rescuer CPR
	Adult obstructed airway
	  conscious
	  unconscious
	Child One-Rescuer CPR
	Child Two-Rescuer CPR
	Child obstructed airway
	  conscious
	  unconscious
	Infant CPR
	Infant obstructed airway
	  conscious
	  unconscious
		Adult one-rescuer CPR
		Adult two-rescuer CPR
		Adult obstructed airway
		  conscious
		  unconscious
		Infant CPR
		Infant obstructed airway
		  conscious
		  unconscious
		Child one-rescuer CPR
		  (optional)
		Child two-rescuer CPR
		  (optional)
		Child obstructed airway
		  conscious (optional)
		  unconscious (optional)
		Cricoid pressure (optional)
		Mouth-to-mask ventilation
		  (optional)

Appendix C: Performance Sheets for Cardiopulmonary Resuscitation and Foreign Body Airway Obstruction Management

BLS Performance Sheet
Adult One-Rescuer CPR

Name _____ Date _____

Step	Objective	Critical Performance	S	U
1. AIRWAY	Assessment: Determine unresponsiveness.	Tap or gently shake shoulder.		
		Shout "Are you OK?"		
	Call for help.	Call out "Help!"		
	Position the victim.	Turn on back as unit, if necessary, supporting head and neck (4–10 sec).		
	Open the airway.	Use head-tilt/chin-lift maneuver.		
2. BREATHING	Assessment: Determine breathlessness.	Maintain open airway.		
		Ear over mouth, observe chest: look, listen, feel for breathing (3–5 sec).		
	Ventilate twice.	Maintain open airway.		
		Seal mouth and nose properly.		
		Ventilate 2 times at 1–1.5 sec/inflation.		
		Observe chest rise (adequate ventilation volume.)		
		Allow deflation between breaths.		
3. CIRCULATION	Assessment: Determine pulselessness.	Feel for carotid pulse on near side of victim (5–10 sec).		
		Maintain head-tilt with other hand.		
	Activate EMS system.	If someone responded to call for help, send him/her to activate EMS system.		
		Total time, Step 1—Activate EMS system: 15–35 sec.		
	Begin chest compressions.	Rescuer kneels by victim's shoulders.		
		Landmark check prior to hand placement.		
		Proper hand position throughout.		
		Rescuer's shoulders over victim's sternum.		
		Equal compression–relaxation.		
		Compress 1½ to 2 inches.		
		Keep hands on sternum during upstroke.		
		Complete chest relaxation on upstroke.		
		Say any helpful mnemonic.		
		Compression rate: 80–100/min (15 per 9–11 sec).		
4. Compression/Ventilation Cycles	Do 4 cycles of 15 compressions and 2 ventilations.	Proper compression/ventilation ratio: 15 compressions to 2 ventilations per cycle.		
		Observe chest rise: 1–1.5 sec/inflation; 4 cycles/52–73 sec.		
5. Reassessment*	Determine pulselessness.	Feel for carotid pulse (5 sec).† If there is no pulse, go to Step 6.		
6. Continue CPR	Ventilate twice.	Ventilate 2 times.		
		Observe chest rise: 1–1.5 sec/inflation.		
	Resume compression/ventilation cycles.	Feel for carotid pulse every few minutes.		

* If 2nd rescuer arrives to replace 1st rescuer: (a) 2nd rescuer identifies self by saying "I know CPR. Can I help?" (b) 2nd rescuer then does pulse check in Step 5 and continues with Step 6. (During practice and testing only one rescuer actually ventilates the manikin. The 2nd rescuer simulates ventilation.) (c) 1st rescuer assesses the adequacy of 2nd rescuer's CPR by observing chest rise during ventilations and by checking the pulse during chest compressions.

† If pulse is present, open airway and check for spontaneous breathing: (a) If breathing is present, maintain open airway and monitor pulse and breathing. (b) If breathing is absent, perform rescue breathing at 12 times/min and monitor pulse.

Instructor _____ Check: Satisfactory _____ Unsatisfactory _____

BLS Performance Sheet
Adult FBAO Management: Conscious

Name _____ Date _____

Step	Objective	Critical Performance	S	U
1. Assessment	Determine airway obstruction.	Ask "Are you choking?"		
		Determine if victim can cough or speak.		
2. Heimlich Maneuver	Perform abdominal thrusts.	Stand behind the victim.		
		Wrap arms around victim's waist.		
		Make a fist with one hand and place the thumb side against victim's abdomen in the midline slightly above the navel and well below the tip of the xiphoid.		
		Grasp fist with the other hand.		
		Press into the victim's abdomen with quick upward thrusts.		
		Each thrust should be distinct and delivered with the intent of relieving the airway obstruction.		
		Repeat thrusts until either the foreign body is expelled or the victim becomes unconscious (see below).		

Victim with Obstructed Airway Becomes Unconscious (Optional Testing Sequence)

Step	Objective	Critical Performance	S	U
3. Positioning	Position the victim.	Turn on back as unit.		
		Place face up, arms by side.		
	Call for help.	Call out "Help!" or, if others respond, activate EMS system.		
4. Foreign Body Check	Perform finger sweep.*	Keep victim's face up.		
		Use tongue–jaw lift to open mouth.		
		Sweep deeply into mouth to remove foreign body.		
5. Breathing Attempt	Ventilate.	Open airway with head-tilt/chin-lift.		
		Seal mouth and nose properly.		
		Attempt to ventilate.		
6. Heimlich Maneuver	(Airway is obstructed.) Perform abdominal thrusts.	Straddle victim's thighs.		
		Place heel of one hand against victim's abdomen, in the midline slightly above the navel and well below the tip of the xiphoid.		
		Place second hand directly on top of first hand.		
		Press into the abdomen with quick upward thrusts.		
		Perform 6–10 abdominal thrusts.		
7. Foreign Body Check	(Airway remains obstructed.) Perform finger sweep.*	Keep victim's face up.		
		Use tongue–jaw lift to open mouth.		
		Sweep deeply into mouth to remove foreign body.		
8. Breathing Attempt	Ventilate.	Open airway with head-tilt/chin-lift.		
		Seal mouth and nose properly.		
		Attempt to ventilate.		
9. Sequencing	(Airway remains obstructed.) Repeat sequence.	Repeat Steps 6–8 until successful.†		

* During practice and testing, simulate finger sweeps.

† After airway obstruction is cleared, ventilate twice and proceed with CPR as indicated.

Instructor _____ Check: Satisfactory _____ Unsatisfactory _____

BLS Performance Sheet
Adult FBAO Management: Unconscious

Name _____ Date _____

Step	Objective	Critical Performance	S	U
1. Assessment	Determine unresponsiveness.	Tap or gently shake shoulder. Shout "Are you OK?"		
	Call for help.	Call out "Help!"		
	Position the victim.	Turn on back as unit, if necessary, supporting head and neck (4–10 sec).		
	Open the airway.	Use head-tilt/chin-lift maneuver.		
	Determine breathlessness.	Maintain open airway.		
		Ear over mouth, observe chest: look, listen, feel for breathing (3–5 sec).		
2. Breathing Attempt	Ventilate.	Maintain open airway.		
		Seal mouth and nose properly.		
		Attempt to ventilate.		
	(Airway is obstructed.) Ventilate.	Reposition victim's head.		
		Seal mouth and nose properly.		
		Reattempt to ventilate.		
	(Airway remains obstructed.) Activate EMS system.	If someone responded to call for help, send him/her to activate EMS system.		
3. Heimlich Maneuver	Perform abdominal thrusts.	Straddle victim's thighs.		
		Place heel of one hand against victim's abdomen in the midline slightly above the navel and well below the tip of the xiphoid.		
		Place second hand directly on top of first hand.		
		Press into the abdomen with quick upward thrusts.		
		Each thrust should be distinct and delivered with the intent of relieving the airway obstruction.		
		Perform 6–10 abdominal thrusts.		
4. Foreign Body Check	Perform finger sweep.*	Keep victim's face up.		
		Use tongue–jaw lift to open mouth.		
		Sweep deeply into mouth to remove foreign body.		
5. Breathing Attempt	Ventilate.	Open airway with head-tilt/chin-lift maneuver.		
		Seal mouth and nose properly.		
		Reattempt to ventilate.		
6. Sequencing	Repeat sequence.	Repeat Steps 3–5 until successful.†		

* During practice and testing simulate finger sweeps.

† After airway obstruction is cleared, ventilate twice and proceed with CPR as indicated.

Instructor _____ Check: Satisfactory _____ Unsatisfactory _____

BLS Performance Sheet
Child One-Rescuer CPR*

Name _____ Date _____

Step	Objective	Critical Performance	S	U
1. AIRWAY	Assessment: Determine unresponsiveness.	Tap or gently shake shoulder.		
		Shout "Are you OK?"		
	Call for help.	Call out "Help!"		
	Position the victim.	Turn on back as unit, if necessary, supporting head and neck (4–10 sec).		
	Open the airway.	Use head-tilt/chin-lift maneuver.		
2. BREATHING	Assessment: Determine breathlessness.	Maintain open airway.		
		Ear over mouth, observe chest: look, listen, feel for breathing (3–5 sec).		
	Ventilate twice.	Maintain open airway.		
		Seal mouth and nose properly.		
		Ventilate 2 times at 1–1.5 sec/inflation.		
		Observe chest rise.		
		Allow deflation between breaths.		
3. CIRCULATION	Assessment: Determine pulselessness.	Feel for carotid pulse on near side of victim (5–10 sec).		
		Maintain head-tilt with other hand.		
	Activate EMS system.	If someone responded to call for help, send him/her to activate EMS system.		
		Total time, Step 1—Activate EMS system: 15–35 sec.		
	Begin chest compressions.	Rescuer kneels by victim's shoulders.		
		Landmark check prior to initial hand placement.§		
		Proper hand position throughout.		
		Rescuer's shoulders over victim's sternum.		
		Equal compression–relaxation.		
		Compress 1 to 1½ inches.		
		Keep hand on sternum during upstroke.		
		Complete chest relaxation on upstroke.		
		Say any helpful mnemonic.		
		Compression rate: 80–100/min (5 per 3–4 sec).		
4. Compression/Ventilation Cycles	Do 10 cycles of 5 compressions and 1 ventilation.	Proper compression/ventilation ratio: 5 compressions to 1 slow ventilation per cycle.		
		Observe chest rise: 1–1.5 sec/inflation (10 cycles/60–87 sec).		
5. Reassessment†	Determine pulselessness.	Feel for carotid pulse (5 sec).‡ If there is no pulse, go to Step 6.		
6. Continue CPR	Ventilate once.	Ventilate one time.		
		Observe chest rise: 1–1.5 sec/inflation.		
	Resume compression/ventilation cycles	Feel for carotid pulse every few minutes.		

* If child is above age of approximately 8 years, the method for adults should be used.

† 2nd rescuer arrives to replace 1st rescuer: (a) 2nd rescuer identifies self by saying "I know CPR. Can I help?" (b) 2nd rescuer then does pulse check in Step 5 and continues with Step 6. (During practice and testing only one rescuer actually ventilates the manikin. The 2nd rescuer simulates ventilation.) (c) 1st rescuer assesses the adequacy of 2nd rescuer's CPR by observing chest rise during ventilations and by checking the pulse during chest compressions.

‡ If pulse is present, open airway and check for spontaneous breathing. (a) If breathing is present, maintain open airway and monitor breathing and pulse. (b) If breathing is absent, perform rescue breathing at 15 times/min and monitor pulse.

§ Thereafter, check hand position visually.

Instructor _____ Check: Satisfactory _____ Unsatisfactory _____

BLS Performance Sheet

Child FBAO Management: Conscious*

Name _____ Date _____

Step	Objective	Critical Performance	S	U
1. Assessment	Determine airway obstruction.*	Ask "Are you choking?"		
		Determine if victim can cough or speak.		
2. Heimlich Maneuver	Perform abdominal thrusts (only if victim's cough is ineffective and there is increasing respiratory difficulty).	Stand behind the victim.		
		Wrap arms around victim's waist.		
		Make a fist with one hand and place the thumb side against victim's abdomen, in the midline slightly above the navel and well below the tip of the xiphoid.		
		Grasp fist with the other hand.		
		Press into the victim's abdomen with quick upward thrusts.		
		Each thrust should be distinct and delivered with the intent of relieving the airway obstruction.		
		Repeat thrusts until either the foreign body is expelled or the victim becomes unconscious (see below).		

Victim with Obstructed Airway Becomes Unconscious (Optional Testing Sequence)

Step	Objective	Critical Performance	S	U
3. Positioning	Position the victim.	Turn on back as unit.		
		Place face up, arms by side.		
	Call for help.	Call out "Help!" or if others respond, activate EMS system.		
4. Foreign Body Check	Manual removal of foreign body if one is found. DO NOT perform blind finger sweep.	Keep victim's face up.		
		Use tongue–jaw lift to open mouth.		
		Look into mouth; remove foreign body ONLY IF VISUALIZED.		
5. Breathing Attempt	Ventilate.	Open airway with head-tilt/chin-lift.		
		Seal mouth and nose properly.		
		Attempt to ventilate.		
6. Heimlich Maneuver	(Airway is obstructed.) Perform abdominal thrusts.	Kneel at victim's feet if on the floor, or stand at victim's feet if on a table.		
		Place heel of one hand against victim's abdomen, in the midline slightly above navel and well below tip of xiphoid.		
		Place second hand directly on top of first hand.		
		Press into the abdomen with quick upward thrusts.		
		Perform 6–10 abdominal thrusts.		
7. Foreign Body Check	(Airway remains obstructed.) Manual removal of foreign body if one is found. DO NOT perform blind finger sweep.	Keep victim's face up.		
		Use tongue–jaw lift to open mouth.		
		Look into mouth; remove foreign body ONLY IF VISUALIZED.		
8. Breathing Attempt	Ventilate.	Open airway with head-tilt/chin-lift.		
		Seal mouth and nose properly.		
		Reattempt to ventilate.		
9. Sequencing	(Airway remains obstructed.) Repeat sequence.	Repeat Steps 6–8 until successful.†		

* This procedure should be initiated in a conscious child only if the airway obstruction is due to a witnessed or strongly suspected aspiration and if respiratory difficulty is increasing and the cough is ineffective. If obstruction is caused by airway swelling due to infection such as epiglottitis or croup, these procedures may be harmful; the child should be rushed to the nearest ALS facility, allowing the child to maintain the position of maximum comfort.

† After airway obstruction is cleared, ventilate twice and proceed with CPR as indicated.

Instructor _____ Check: Satisfactory _____ Unsatisfactory _____

BLS Performance Sheet

Child FBAO Management: Unconscious

Name _____ Date _____

Step	Objective	Critical Performance	S	U
1. Assessment	Determine unresponsiveness.	Tap or gently shake shoulder.		
		Shout "Are you OK?"		
	Call for help.	Call out "Help!"		
	Position the victim.	Turn on back as unit, if necessary, supporting head and neck (4–10 sec).		
	Open the airway.	Use head-tilt/chin-lift maneuver.		
	Determine breathlessness.	Maintain open airway.		
		Ear over mouth, observe chest: look, listen, feel for breathing (3–5 sec).		
2. Breathing Attempt	Ventilate.	Maintain open airway.		
		Seal mouth and nose properly.		
		Attempt to ventilate.		
	(Airway is obstructed.) Ventilate.	Reposition victim's head.		
		Seal mouth and nose properly.		
		Reattempt to ventilate.		
	(Airway remains obstructed.) Activate EMS system.	If someone responded to call for help, send him/her to activate EMS system.		
3. Heimlich Maneuver	Perform abdominal thrusts.	Kneel at victim's feet if on the floor, or stand at victim's feet if on a table.		
		Place heel of one hand against victim's abdomen in the midline slightly above navel and well below tip of xiphoid.		
		Place second hand directly on top of first hand.		
		Press into the abdomen with quick upward thrusts.		
		Each thrust should be distinct and delivered with the intent of relieving the airway.		
		Perform 6–10 abdominal thrusts.		
4. Foreign Body Check	(Airway remains obstructed.) Manual removal of foreign body if one is found. DO NOT perform blind finger sweep.	Keep victim's face up.		
		Use tongue–jaw lift to open mouth.		
		Look into mouth; remove foreign body ONLY IF VISUALIZED.		
5. Breathing Attempt	Ventilate.	Open airway with head-tilt/chin-lift maneuver.		
		Seal mouth and nose properly.		
		Reattempt to ventilate.		
6. Sequencing	Repeat sequence.	Repeat Steps 3–5 until successful.*		

* After airway obstruction is cleared, ventilate twice and proceed with CPR as indicated.

Instructor _____ Check: Satisfactory _____ Unsatisfactory _____

BLS Performance Sheet
Infant CPR

Name _____ Date _____

Step	Objective	Critical Performance	S	U
1. AIRWAY	Assessment: Determine unresponsiveness.	Tap or gently shake shoulder.		
	Call for help.	Call out "Help!"		
	Position the infant.	Turn on back as unit, supporting head and neck.		
		Place on firm, hard surface.		
	Open the airway.	Use head-tilt/chin-lift maneuver to sniffing or neutral position.		
		Do not overextend the head.		
2. BREATHING	Assessment: Determine breathlessness.	Maintain open airway.		
		Ear over mouth, observe chest: look, listen, feel for breathing (3–5 sec).		
	Ventilate twice.	Maintain open airway.		
		Make tight seal on infant's mouth and nose with rescuer's mouth.		
		Ventilate 2 times at 1–1.5 sec/inflation.		
		Observe chest rise.		
		Allow deflation between breaths.		
3. CIRCULATION	Assessment: Determine pulselessness.	Feel for brachial pulse (5–10 sec).		
		Maintain head-tilt with other hand.		
	Activate EMS system.	If someone responded to call for help, send him/her to activate EMS system.		
		Total time, Step 1—Activate EMS system: 15–35 sec.		
	Begin chest compressions.	Imagine line between nipples (intermammary line).		
		Place 2–3 fingers on sternum, 1 finger's width below intermammary line.		
		Equal compression–relaxation.		
		Compress vertically, ½ to 1 inches.		
		Keep fingers on sternum during upstroke.		
		Complete chest relaxation on upstroke.		
		Say any helpful mnemonic.		
		Compression rate: at least 100/min (5 in 3 sec or less).		
4. Compression/Ventilation Cycles	Do 10 cycles of 5 compressions and 1 ventilation.	Proper compression/ventilation ratio: 5 compressions to 1 slow ventilation per cycle.		
		Pause for ventilation.		
		Observe chest rise: 1–1.5 sec/inflation 10 cycles/45 sec or less.		
5. Reassessment	Determine pulselessness.	Feel for brachial pulse (5 sec).* If there is no pulse, go to Step 6.		
6. Continue CPR	Ventilate once.	Ventilate 1 time.		
		Observe chest rise: 1–1.5 sec/inflation.		
	Resume compression/ventilation cycles.	Feel for brachial pulse every few minutes.		

* If pulse is present, open airway and check for spontaneous breathing. (a) If breathing is present, maintain open airway and monitor breathing and pulse. (b) If breathing is absent, perform rescue breathing at 20 times/min and monitor pulse.

Instructor _____ Check: Satisfactory _____ Unsatisfactory _____

BLS Performance Sheet
Infant FBAO Management: Conscious*

Name _____ Date _____

Step	Objective	Critical Performance	S	U
1. Assessment	Determine airway obstruction.*	Observe breathing difficulties.*		
2. Back Blows	Deliver 4 back blows.	Supporting head and neck with one hand, straddle infant face down, head lower than trunk, over your forearm supported on your thigh.		
		Deliver 4 back blows, forcefully, between the shoulder blades with the heel of the hand (3–5 sec).		
3. Chest Thrusts	Deliver 4 chest thrusts.	While supporting the head, sandwich infant between your hands and turn on back, with head lower than trunk.		
		Deliver 4 thrusts in the midsternal region in the same manner as external chest compressions, but at a slower rate (3–5 sec).		
4. Sequencing	Repeat sequence.	Repeat Steps 2 and 3 until either the foreign body is expelled or the infant becomes unconscious (see below).		

Infant with Obstructed Airway Becomes Unconscious (Optional Testing Sequence)

Step	Objective	Critical Performance	S	U
5. Call for Help.	Call for help.	Call out "Help!" or, if others respond, activate EMS system.		
6. Foreign Body Check	Manual removal of foreign body if one is found (tongue–jaw lift, NOT blind finger sweep).	Keep victim's face up.		
		Place thumb in infant's mouth, over tongue. Lift tongue and jaw forward with fingers wrapped around lower jaw.		
		Look into mouth; remove foreign body ONLY IF VISUALIZED.		
7. Breathing Attempt	Ventilate.	Open airway with head-tilt/chin-lift.		
		Seal mouth and nose properly.		
		Attempt to ventilate.		
8. Back Blows	(Airway is obstructed.) Deliver 4 back blows.	Supporting head and neck with one hand, straddle infant face down, head lower than trunk, over your forearm supported on your thigh.		
		Deliver 4 back blows, forcefully, between the shoulder blades with the heel of the hand (3–5 sec).		
9. Chest Thrusts	Deliver 4 chest thrusts.	While supporting the head and neck, sandwich infant between your hands and turn on back, with head lower than trunk.		
		Deliver 4 thrusts in the midsternal region in the same manner as external chest compressions, but at a slower rate (3–5 sec).		
10. Foreign Body Check	(Airway remains obstructed.) Manual removal of foreign body if one is found.	Keep victim's face up.		
		Do tongue–jaw lift, but NOT blind finger sweep.		
		Look into mouth, remove foreign body ONLY IF VISUALIZED.		
11. Breathing Attempt	Ventilate.	Open airway with head-tilt/chin-lift.		
		Seal mouth and nose properly.		
		Reattempt to ventilate.		
12. Sequencing	(Airway remains obstructed.) Repeat sequence.	Repeat Steps 8–11 until successful.†		

* This procedure should be initiated in a conscious infant only if the airway obstruction is due to a witnessed or strongly suspected aspiration and if respiratory difficulty is increasing and the cough is ineffective. If the obstruction is caused by airway swelling due to infections, such as epiglottitis or croup, these procedures may be harmful; the infant should be rushed to the nearest ALS facility, allowing the infant to maintain the position of maximum comfort.

† After airway obstruction is cleared, ventilate twice and proceed with CPR as indicated.

Instructor _____ Check: Satisfactory _____ Unsatisfactory _____

BLS Performance Sheet

Infant FBAO Management: Unconscious

Name _____ Date _____

Step	Objective	Critical Performance	S	U
1. Assessment	Determine unresponsiveness.	Tap or gently shake shoulder.		
	Call for help.	Call out "Help!"		
	Position the infant.	Turn on back as unit, if necessary, supporting head and neck.		
		Place on firm, hard surface.		
	Open the airway.	Use head-tilt/chin-lift maneuver to sniffing or neutral position.		
		Do not overextend the head.		
	Determine breathlessness.	Maintain open airway.		
		Ear over mouth, observe chest: look, listen, feel for breathing (3–5 sec).		
2. Breathing Attempt	Ventilate.	Maintain open airway.		
		Make tight seal on mouth and nose of infant with rescuer's mouth.		
		Attempt to ventilate.		
	(Airway is obstructed.) Ventilate.	Reposition infant's head.		
		Seal mouth and nose properly.		
		Reattempt to ventilate.		
	(Airway remains obstructed.) Activate EMS system	If someone responded to call for help, send him/her to activate EMS system.		
3. Back Blows	Deliver 4 back blows.	Supporting head and neck with one hand, straddle infant face down, head lower than trunk, over your forearm supported on your thigh.		
		Deliver 4 back blows, forcefully, between the shoulder blades with the heel of the hand (3–5 sec).		
4. Chest Thrusts	Deliver 4 chest thrusts.	While supporting the head and neck, sandwich infant between your hands and turn on back, with head lower than trunk.		
		Deliver 4 thrusts in the midsternal region in the same manner as external chest compressions, but at a slower rate (3–5 sec).		
5. Foreign Body Check	(Airway remains obstructed.) Manual removal of foreign body if one is found (tongue–jaw lift, NOT blind finger sweep).	Keep victim's face up.		
		Place thumb in infant's mouth, over tongue. Lift tongue and jaw forward with fingers wrapped around lower jaw.		
		Look into mouth; remove foreign body ONLY IF VISUALIZED.		
6. Breathing Attempt	Ventilate.	Open airway with head-tilt/chin-lift.		
		Seal mouth and nose properly.		
		Reattempt to ventilate.		
7. Sequencing	Repeat sequence.	Repeat Steps 3–6 until successful.*		

* After airway obstruction is cleared, ventilate twice and proceed with CPR as indicated.

Instructor _____ Check: Satisfactory _____ Unsatisfactory _____

BLS Performance Sheet
Adult Two-Rescuer CPR*

Name _____ Date _____

Step	Objective	Critical Performance	S	U
1. AIRWAY	**One rescuer (ventilator):** Assessment: Determine unresponsiveness.	Tap or gently shake shoulder.		
		Shout "Are you OK?"		
	Position the victim.	Turn on back if necessary (4–10 sec).		
	Open the airway.	Use a proper technique to open airway.		
2. BREATHING	Assessment: Determine breathlessness.	Look, listen, and feel (3–5 sec).		
	Ventilate twice.	Observe chest rise: 1–1.5 sec/inflation.		
3. CIRCULATION	Assessment: Determine pulselessness.	Feel for carotid pulse (5–10 sec).		
	State assessment results.	Say "No pulse."		
	Other rescuer (compressor): Get into position for compressions.	Hands, shoulders in correct position.		
	Locate landmark notch.	Landmark check.		
4. Compression/Ventilation Cycles	**Compressor:** Begin chest compressions.	Correct ratio compressions/ventilations: 5/1.		
		Compression rate: 80–100/min (5 compressions/3–4 sec).		
		Say any helpful mnemonic.		
		Stop compressing for each ventilation.		
	Ventilator: Ventilate after every 5th compression and check compression effectiveness.	Ventilate 1 time (1–1.5 sec/inflation).		
		Check pulse occasionally to assess compressions.		
	(Minimum of 10 cycles.)	Time for 10 cycles: 40–53 sec.		
5. Call for Switch	**Compressor:** Call for switch when fatigued.	Give clear signal to change.		
		Compressor completes 5th compression.		
		Ventilator completes ventilation after 5th compression.		
6. Switch	Simultaneously switch:			
	Ventilator: Move to chest.	Move to chest.		
		Become compressor.		
		Get into position for compressions.		
		Locate landmark notch.		
	Compressor: Move to head.	Move to head.		
		Become ventilator.		
		Check carotid pulse (5 sec).		
		Say "No pulse."		
		Ventilate once (1–1.5 sec/inflation).†		
7. Continue CPR	Resume compression/ventilation cycles.	Resume Step 4.		

* (a) If CPR is in progress with one rescuer (lay person), the entrance of the two rescuers occurs after the completion of one rescuer's cycle of 15 compressions and 2 ventilations. The EMS should be activated first. The two new rescuers start with Step 6. (b) If CPR is in progress with one healthcare provider, the entrance of a second healthcare provider is at the end of a cycle after check for pulse by first rescuer. The new cycle starts with one ventilation by the first rescuer, and the second rescuer becomes the compressor.

† During practice and testing only one rescuer actually ventilates the manikin. The other rescuer simulates ventilation.

Instructor _____ Check: Satisfactory _____ Unsatisfactory _____

BLS Performance Sheet
Child Two-Rescuer CPR*

Name _____ Date _____

Step	Objective	Critical Performance	S	U
1. AIRWAY	One rescuer (ventilator): Assessment: Determine unresponsiveness.	Tap or gently shake shoulder.		
		Shout "Are you OK?"		
	Position the victim.	Turn on back if necessary (4–10 sec).		
	Open the airway.	Use a proper technique to open airway.		
2. BREATHING	Assessment: Determine breathlessness.	Look, listen, and feel (3–5 sec).		
	Ventilate twice.	Observe chest rise: 1–1.5 sec/inflation.		
3. CIRCULATION	Assessment: Determine pulselessness.	Feel for carotid pulse (5–10 sec).		
	State assessment results.	Say "No pulse."		
	Other rescuer (compressor): Get into position for compressions.	Hand, shoulders in correct position.		
	Locate landmark notch.	Landmark check.		
4. Compression/Ventilation Cycles	Compressor: Begin chest compressions.	Correct ratio compressions/ventilations: 5/1.		
		Compression rate: 80–100/min (5 compressions/3–4 sec).		
		Say any helpful mnemonic.		
		Stop compressing for each ventilation.		
	Ventilator: Ventilate after every 5th compression and check compression effectiveness.	Ventilate 1 time (1–1.5 sec/inflation).		
		Check pulse occasionally to assess compressions.		
	(Minimum of 10 cycles.)	Time for 10 cycles: 40–53 sec.		
5. Call for Switch	Compressor: Call for switch when fatigued.	Give clear signal to change.		
		Compressor completes 5th compression.		
		Ventilator completes ventilation after 5th compression.		
6. Switch	Simultaneously switch:			
	Ventilator: Move to chest.	Move to chest.		
		Become compressor.		
		Get into position for compressions.		
		Locate landmark notch.		
	Compressor: Move to head.	Move to head.		
		Become ventilator.		
		Check carotid pulse (5 sec).		
		Say "No pulse."		
		Ventilate once (1–1.5 sec/inflation).†		
7. Continue CPR	Resume compression/ventilation cycles.	Resume Step 4.		

* (a) If CPR is in progress with one rescuer (layperson), the entrance of the two rescuers occurs after the completion of one rescuer's cycle of 5 compressions and 1 ventilation. The EMS should be activated first. The two new rescuers start with Step 6. (b) If CPR is in progress with one healthcare provider, the entrance of a second healthcare provider is at the end of a cycle after check for pulse by first rescuer. The new cycle starts with one ventilation by the first rescuer, and the second rescuer becomes the compressor.

† During practice and testing only one rescuer actually ventilates the manikin. The other rescuer simulates ventilation.

Instructor _____ Check: Satisfactory _____ Unsatisfactory _____

BLS Summary Performance Sheet
Cardiopulmonary Resuscitation (CPR)

	Objectives	Actions		
		Adult (over 8 yrs.)	**Child** (1 to 8 yrs.)	**Infant** (under 1 yr.)
A. Airway	1. Assessment: Determine unresponsiveness.	Tap or gently shake shoulder.		
		Say, "Are you okay?"		Observe
	2. Get help.	Call out "Help!"		
	3. Position the victim.	Turn on back as a unit, supporting head and neck if necessary. (4–10 seconds)		
	4. Open the airway.	Head-tilt/chin-lift		
B. Breathing	5. Assessment: Determine breathlessness.	Maintain open airway. Place ear over mouth, observing chest. Look, listen, feel for breathing. (3–5 seconds)		
	6. Give 2 rescue breaths.	Maintain open airway.		
		Seal mouth to mouth		Mouth to nose/mouth
		Give 2 rescue breaths, 1 to 1½ seconds per inflation. Observe chest rise. Allow lung deflation between breaths.		
	7. Option for obstructed airway	a. Reposition victim's head. Try again to give rescue breaths.		
		b. Activate the EMS system.		
		c. Give 6–10 subdiaphragmatic abdominal thrusts (the Heimlich maneuver).		Give 4 back blows.
				Give 4 chest thrusts.
		d. Tongue–jaw lift and finger sweep	Tongue–jaw lift, but finger sweep only if you see a foreign object.	
		If unsuccessful, repeat a, c, and d until successful.		
C. Circulation	8. Assessment: Determine pulselessness.	Feel for carotid pulse with one hand; maintain head-tilt with the other. (5–10 seconds)		Feel for brachial pulse; keep head-tilt.
	9. Activate EMS system.	If someone responded to call for help, send them to activate the EMS system.		
	Begin chest compressions: 10. Landmark check	Run middle finger along bottom edge of rib cage to notch at center (tip of sternum).		Imagine a line drawn between the nipples.
	11. Hand position	Place index finger next to finger on notch:		Place 2–3 fingers on sternum, 1 finger's width below line. Depress ½–1 in.
		Two hands next to index finger. Depress 1½–2 in.	Heel of one hand next to index finger. Depress 1–1½ in.	
	12. Compression rate	80–100 per minute		At least 100 per minute
CPR Cycles	13. Compressions to breaths.	2 breaths to every 15 compressions.	1 breath to every 5 compressions.	
	14. Number of cycles.	4 (52–73 seconds)	10 (60–87 seconds)	10 (45 seconds or less)
	15. Reassessment.	Feel for carotid pulse. (5 seconds)		Feel for brachial pulse.
		If no pulse, resume CPR, starting with 2 breaths.	If no pulse, resume CPR, starting with 1 breath.	
Option for entrance of 2nd rescuer: "I know CPR. Can I help?"	1st rescuer ends CPR.	End cycle with 2 rescue breaths.	End cycle with 1 rescue breath.	
	2nd rescuer checks pulse (5 seconds).	Feel for carotid pulse.		Feel for brachial pulse.
	If no pulse, 2nd rescuer begins CPR.	Begin one-rescuer CPR, starting with 2 breaths.	Begin one-rescuer CPR, starting with 1 breath.	
	1st rescuer monitors 2nd rescuer.	Watch for chest rise and fall during rescue breathing; check pulse during chest compressions.		
Option for pulse return	If no breathing, give rescue breaths.	1 breath every 5 seconds	1 breath every 4 seconds	1 breath every 3 seconds

BLS Summary Performance Sheet
Foreign Body Airway Obstruction Management

	Objectives	Actions		
		Adult (over 8 yrs.)	**Child** (1 to 8 yrs.)	**Infant** (under 1 yr.)
Conscious Victim	**1.** Assessment: Determine airway obstruction.	Ask, "Are you choking?" Determine if victim can cough or speak.		Observe breathing difficulty.
	2. Act to relieve obstruction.	Perform subdiaphragmatic abdominal thrusts (Heimlich maneuver 6–10 repetitions).		Give 4 back blows.
				Give 4 chest thrusts.
	Be persistent.	Repeat Step 2 until obstruction is relieved or victim becomes unconscious.		
Victim Who Becomes Unconscious	**3.** Position the victim; call for help.	Turn on back as a unit, supporting head and neck, face up, arms by sides. Call out, "Help!" If others come, activate EMS.		
	4. Check for foreign body.	Perform tongue–jaw lift and finger sweep.	Perform tongue–jaw lift. Remove foreign object only if you actually see it.	
	5. Give rescue breaths.	Open the airway with head-tilt/chin-lift. Try to give rescue breaths.		
	6. Act to relieve obstruction.	Perform subdiaphragmatic abdominal thrusts (Heimlich maneuver 6–10 repetitions).		Give 4 back blows.
				Give 4 chest thrusts.
	7. Check for foreign body.	Perform tongue–jaw lift and finger sweep.	Perform tongue–jaw lift. Remove foreign object only if you actually see it.	
	8. Try again to give rescue breaths.	Open the airway with head-tilt/chin-lift. Try to give rescue breaths.		
	9. Be persistent.	Repeat Steps 6–8 until obstruction is relieved.		
Unconscious Victim	**1.** Assessment: Determine unresponsiveness.	Tap or gently shake shoulder. Shout, "Are you okay?"		Tap or gently shake shoulder.
	2. Call for help; position the victim.	Turn on back as a unit, supporting head and neck, face up, arms by sides. Call out, "Help!" If others come, activate EMS.		
	3. Open the airway.	Head-tilt/chin-lift		Head-tilt/chin-lift, but do not tilt too far.
	4. Assessment: Determine breathlessness	Maintain an open airway. Ear over mouth; observe chest. Look, listen, feel for breathing. (3–5 seconds)		
	5. Give rescue breaths.	Make mouth-to-mouth seal.		Make mouth-to-nose-and-mouth seal.
		Try to give rescue breaths.		
	6. Try again to give rescue breaths.	Reposition head. Try rescue breaths again.		
	7. Activate the EMS system.	If someone responded to the call for help, that person should activate the EMS system.		
	8. Act to relieve obstruction.	Perform subdiaphragmatic abdominal thrusts (Heimlich maneuver 6–10 repetitions).		Give 4 back blows.
				Give 4 chest thrusts.
	9. Check for foreign body.	Perform tongue–jaw lift and finger sweep.	Perform tongue–jaw lift. Remove foreign object only if you actually see it.	
	10. Rescue breaths.	Open the airway with head-tilt/chin-lift. Try again to give rescue breaths.		
	11. Be persistent.	Repeat Steps 8–10 until obstruction is relieved.		